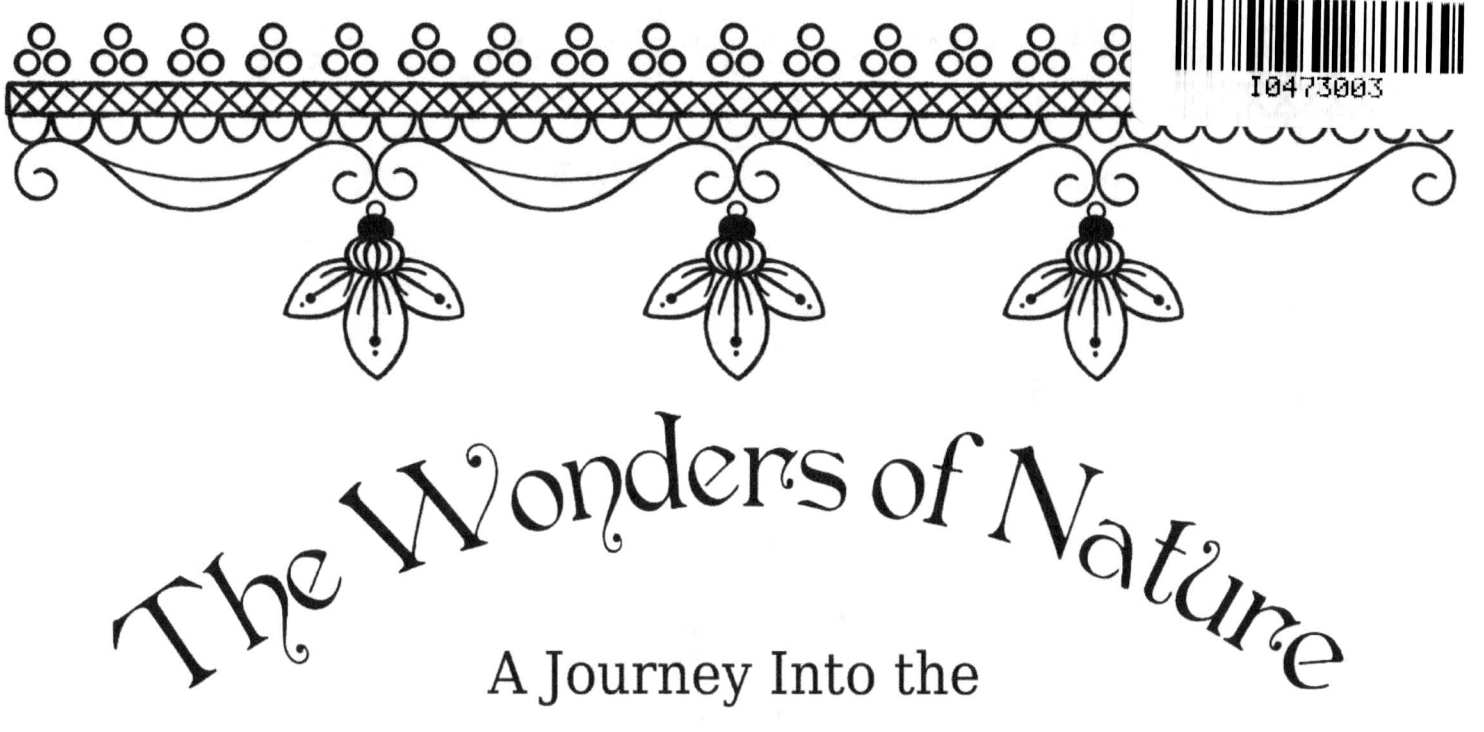

The Wonders of Nature

A Journey Into the
World of Mehndi Henna with a *Twist*

by Olivia A Kneibler
Editor: Chase A Stump

ISBN: 978-0-9995686-0-6

Published in the United States of America in 2017 by Alexandrienne

Image Contents

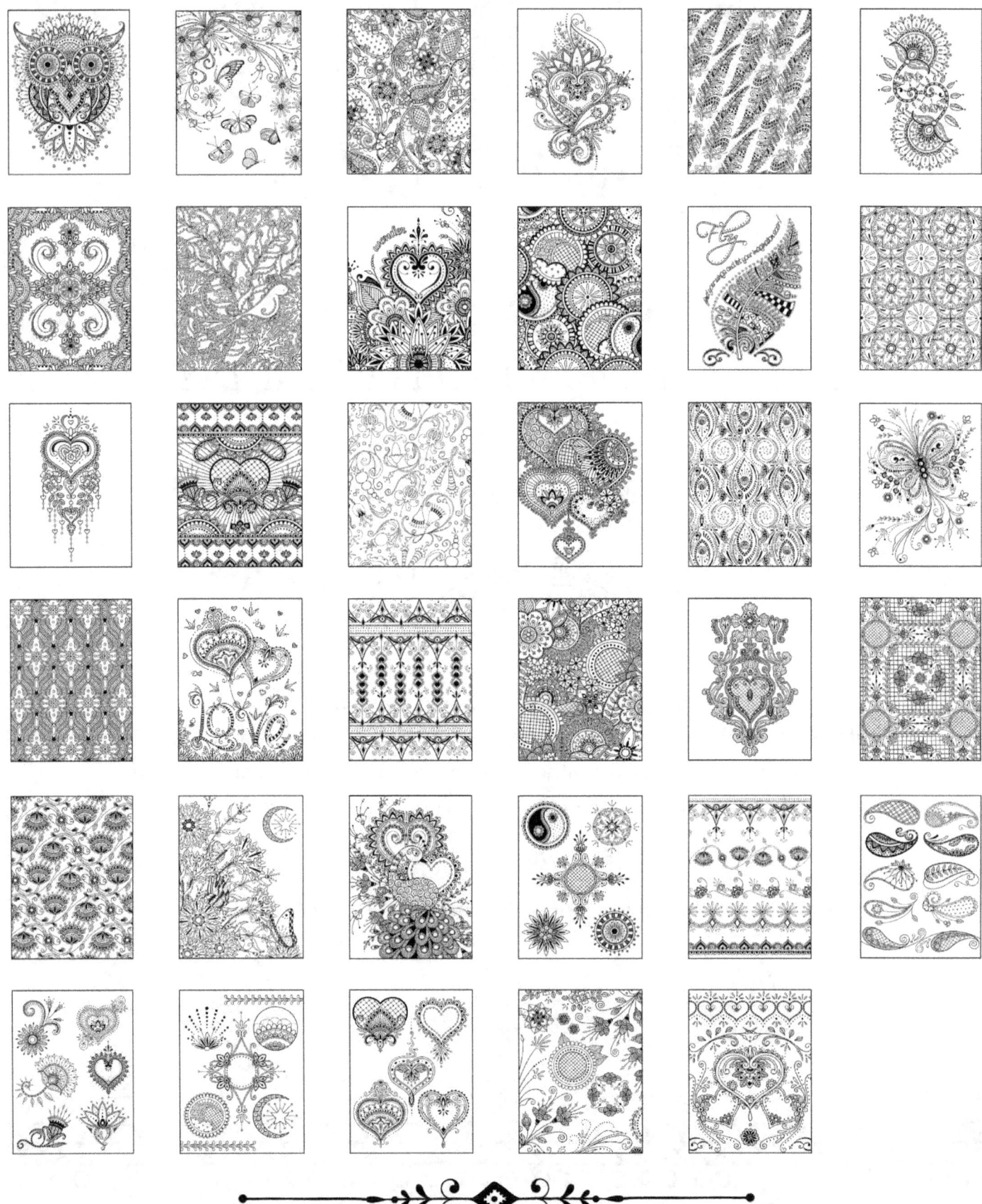

About The Wonders of Nature

In today's fast paced world we need time to slow down so we can unwind, relax, and allow our inner creativity to flow. Once you open this book and begin your journey, you'll be able to leave the chaos behind and enjoy the world of relaxing creativity. Within these pages you are free to make all of the choices that bring you joy.

The Wonders of Nature is a whimsical coloring book containing original illustrations of nature's flowers with a bit of a twist - just for fun. The Mehndi style fits in perfectly with my love of lighthearted doodles, dangles, tangles, and such. It's because of my fascination with these art styles that I was inspired to create this book and share it with you. Each design was created by hand with just a few of them having any computer aided elements. I have combined these designs in fun and interesting ways resulting in the finished images you'll find in the first 27 coloring pages.

Many people refer to this type of art as henna because of the plant that is used to create Mehndi style temporary tattoos. For those pondering the idea of getting a tattoo this book may be the perfect resource for you. There are over 30 designs included that can be used as templates for adorning your body with henna.

The Last 8 Coloring Pages

In this section the designs are meant to be colored but they can be turned into much more than that. In addition to coloring this section can turn into a fun adventure. Within these pages you will find tattooing templates, a game, and a starting point for you to draw as well as color your very own Mehndi images. Whether you want some relaxing color time or the thrill of creation you'll find it here. These pages contain elements that were used to create the completed images as well as some designs that you won't find anywhere else in the book.

Enjoy the Possibilities!

• Use the designs as templates in case you would like to try henna tattooing.
• Make a fun road trip game. Can you find any of these designs in the finished images?
• Create your own finished images for coloring by using these designs and the last two image pages of this book as a guide. These designs will give you a starting point which will help you to turn your ideas into reality. Simply select some designs you like, combine them in a way that pleases you or use them simply as a guide and create your own finished coloring pages in your personal creative style.

You've Spoken & I've Listened

Research has taught me that you, the colorist, would like to have some items included in your coloring books. Because you've voiced your desires I've incorporated them to the best of my ability.

In The Wonders of Nature you will find:

One blank page for testing colors and media types, also for doodling patterns and designs that you might want to incorporate into the images.

All coloring pages are one sided with the back sides left blank. This is so you can color every page without having to choose between them.

All images are framed with plenty of outside space so you shouldn't have to worry about tearing the image if you are removing it from the book.

A wide range of challenge levels from very easy to rather challenging. I've read that unless someone is searching for a particular level of difficulty they prefer the coloring book to have a variety of challenges.

Suggestions - Both Technical & Artistic

I strongly suggest you put a piece of card stock behind the image you are coloring. This adds some padding for possible bleed through for wet media as well as keeping the next page from having indentations from pushing hard with your colored pencils.

Test first if you are considering wet media; try it on the blank page that's provided to see if it meets with your expectations.

Dry media will not be subject to bleed through which makes it the obvious choice if you have any doubts.

If you want to add patterns to an image, do it. If you want to add an element like a butterfly, go right ahead, in fact I encourage you to do that. Express your personality by coloring, drawing, experimenting and most of all by having some creative fun!

Don't stress over everything being perfect; enjoy the process itself, let your mind wonder on the beauty and creativity you are here to experience.

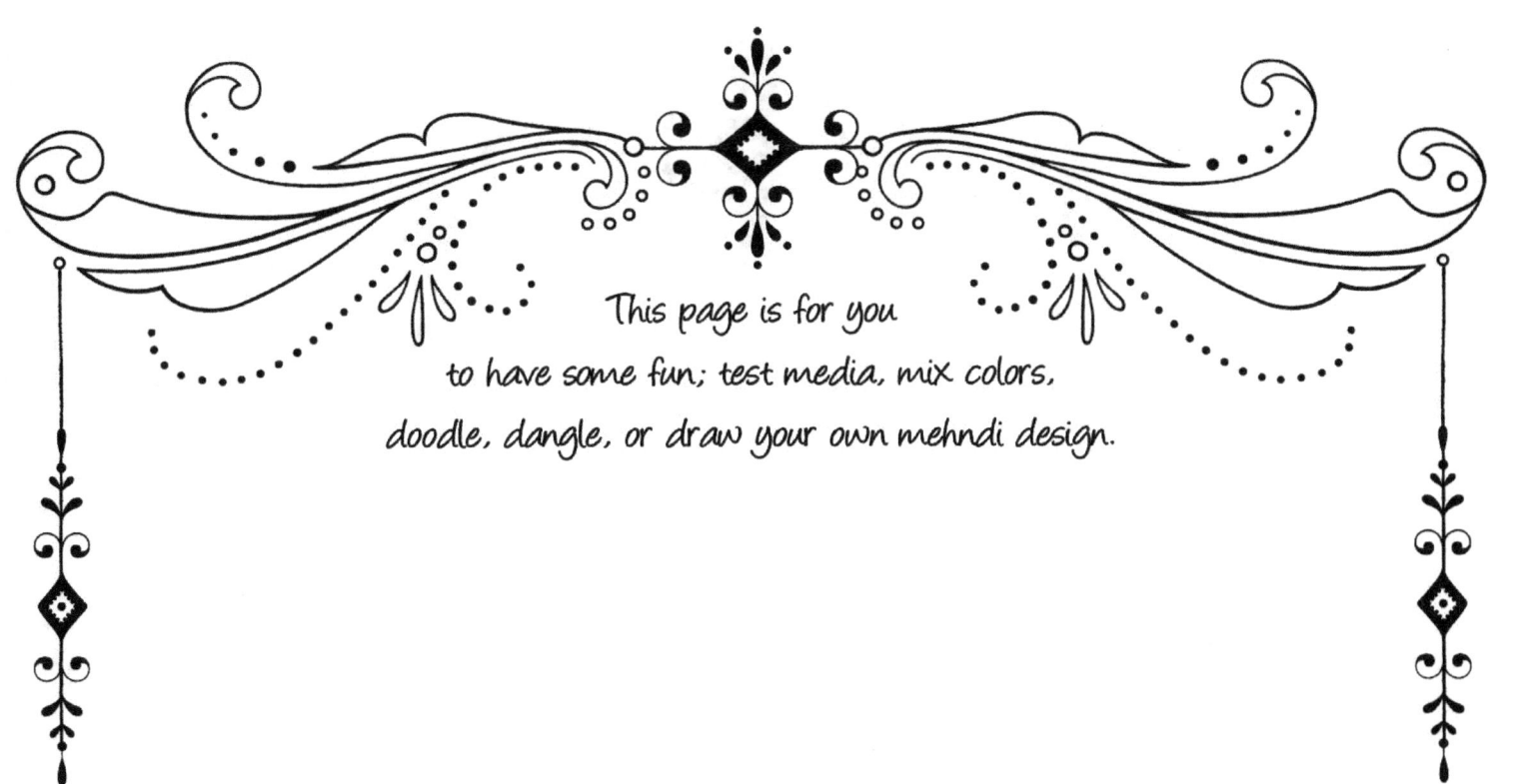

This page is for you
to have some fun; test media, mix colors,
doodle, dangle, or draw your own mehndi design.

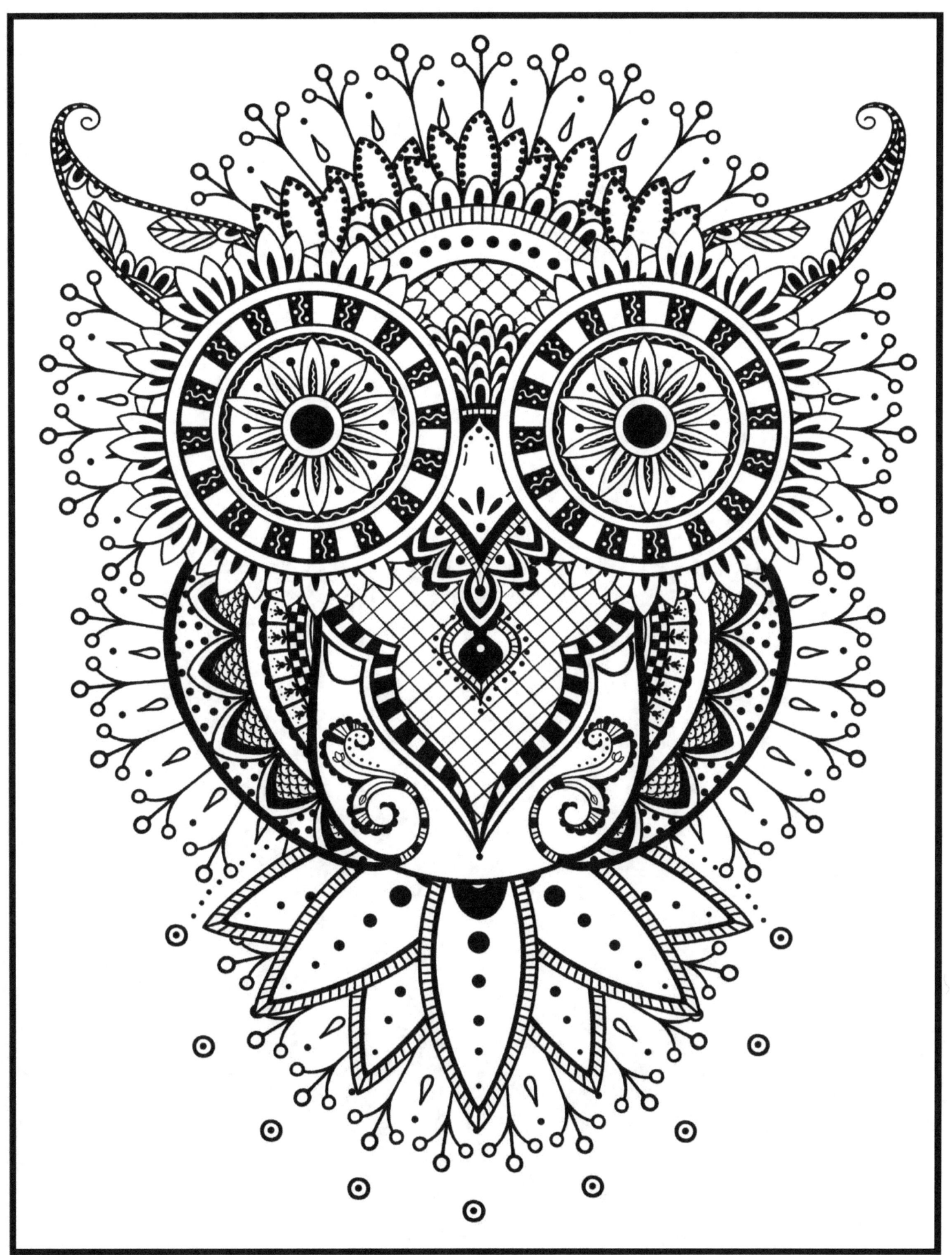

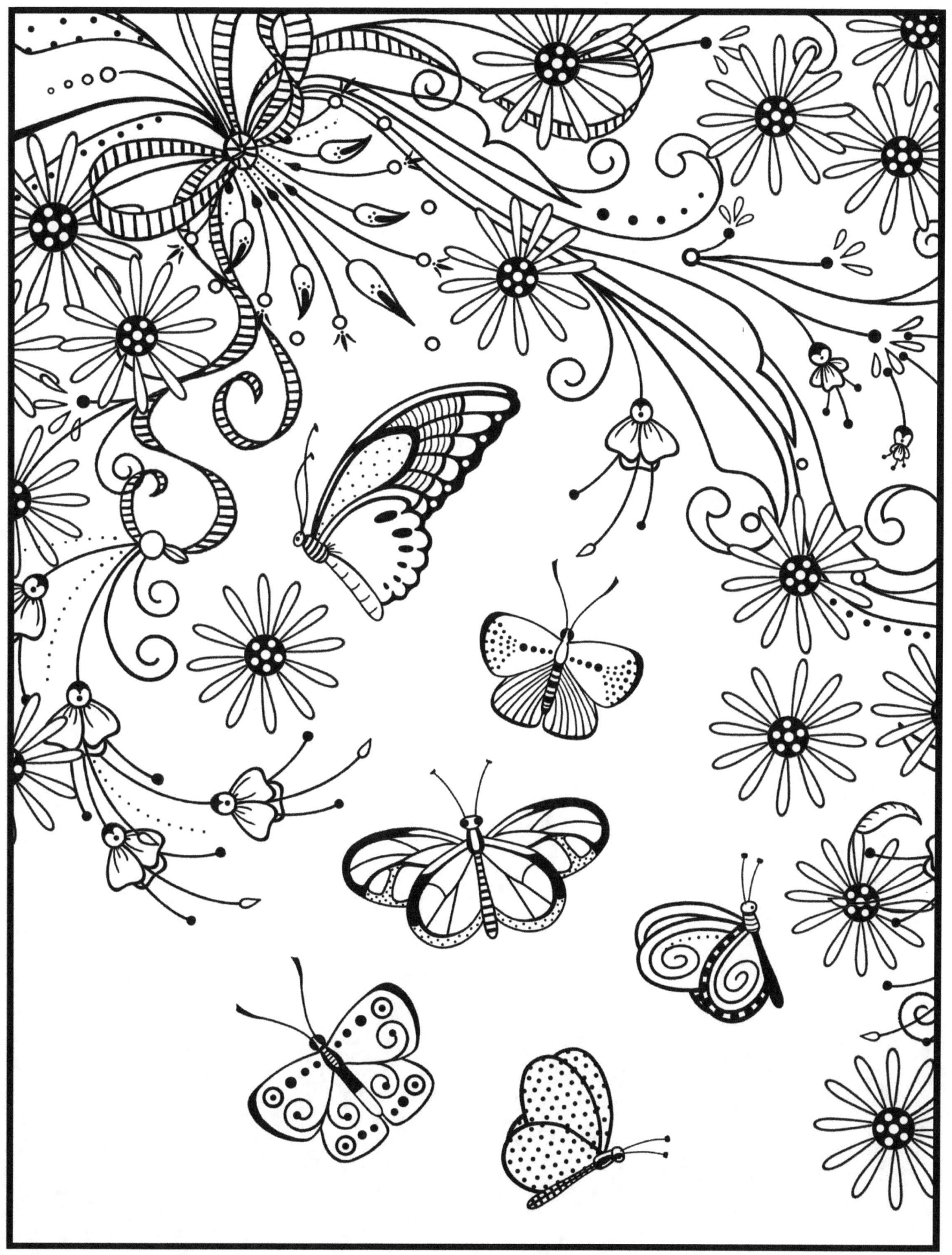

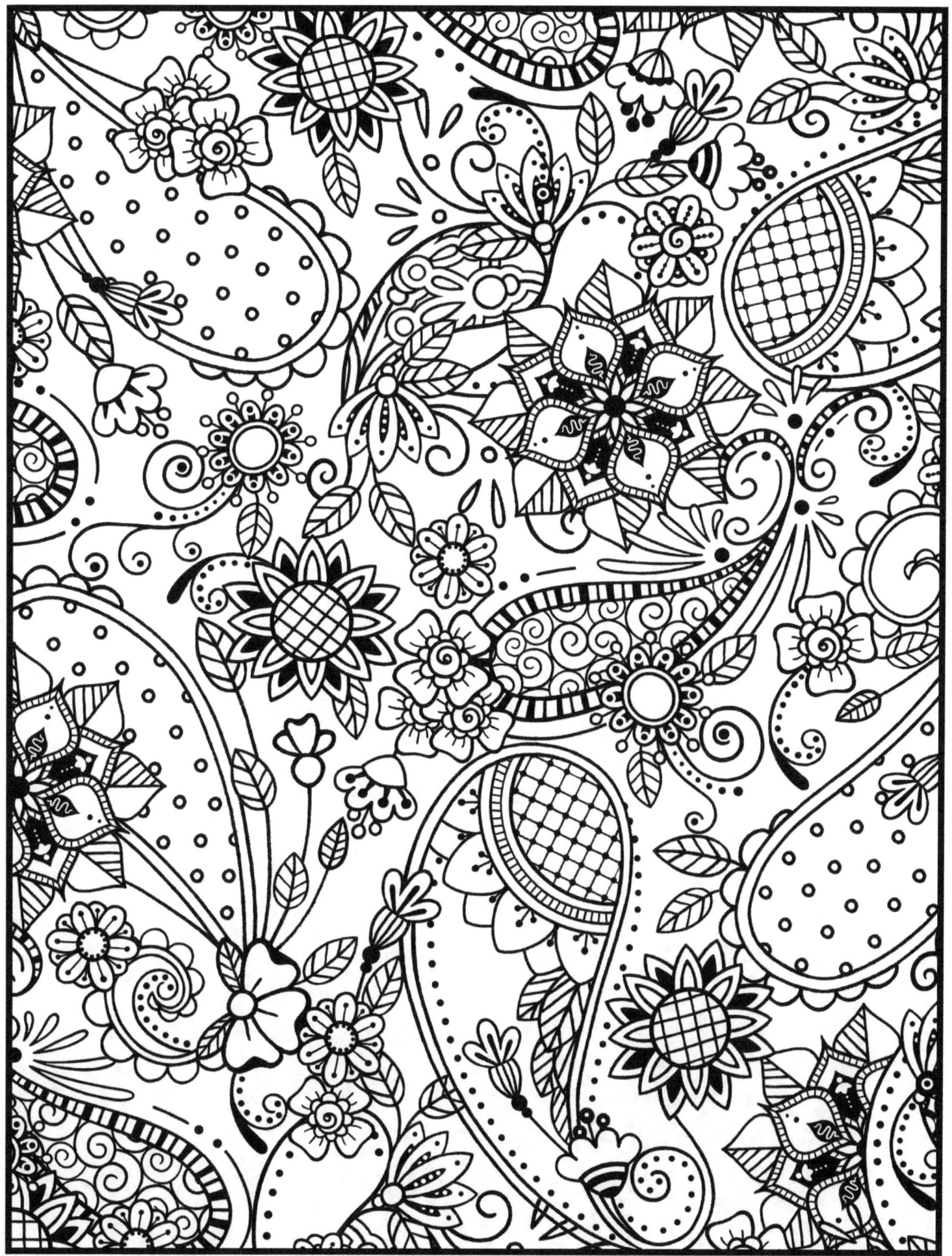

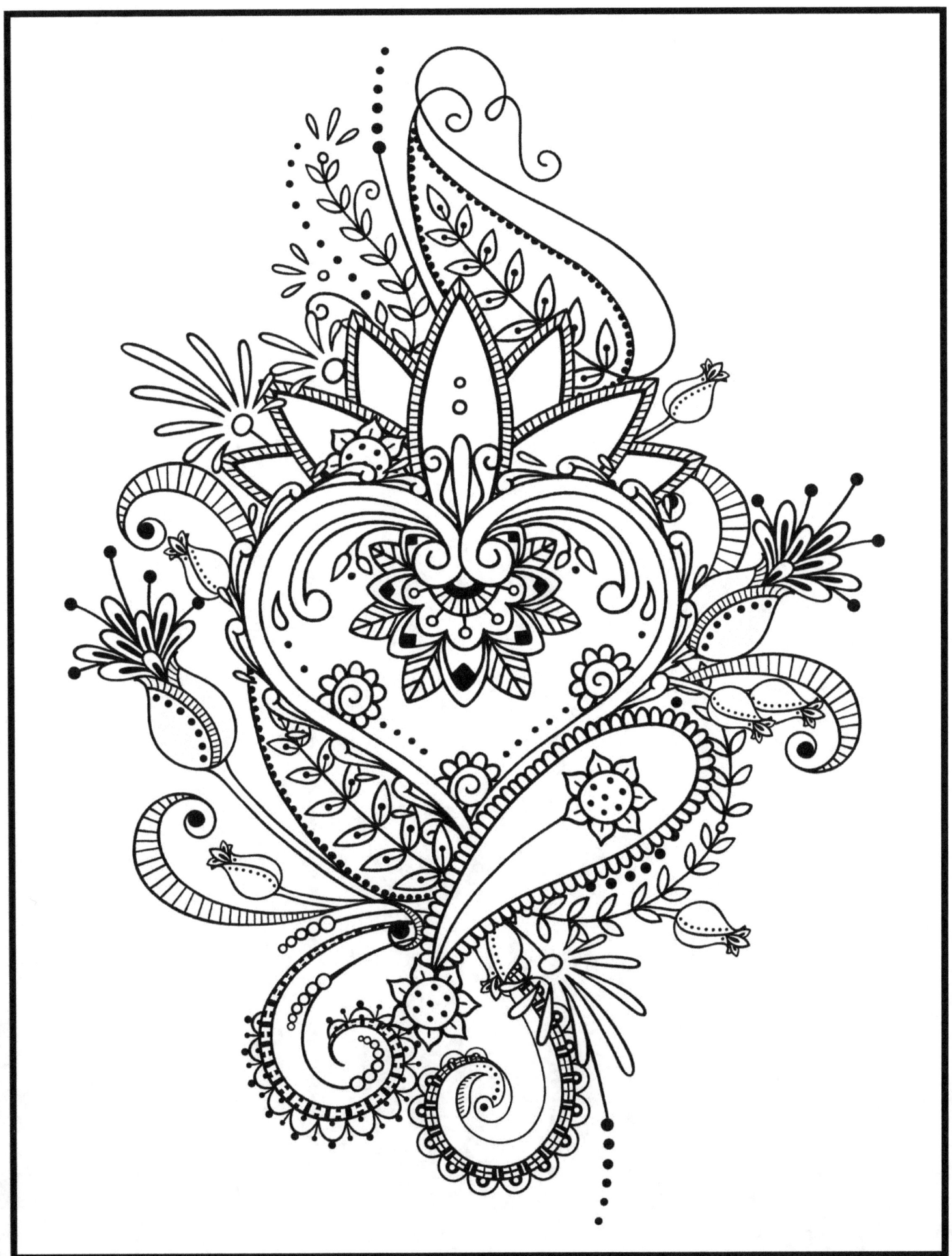

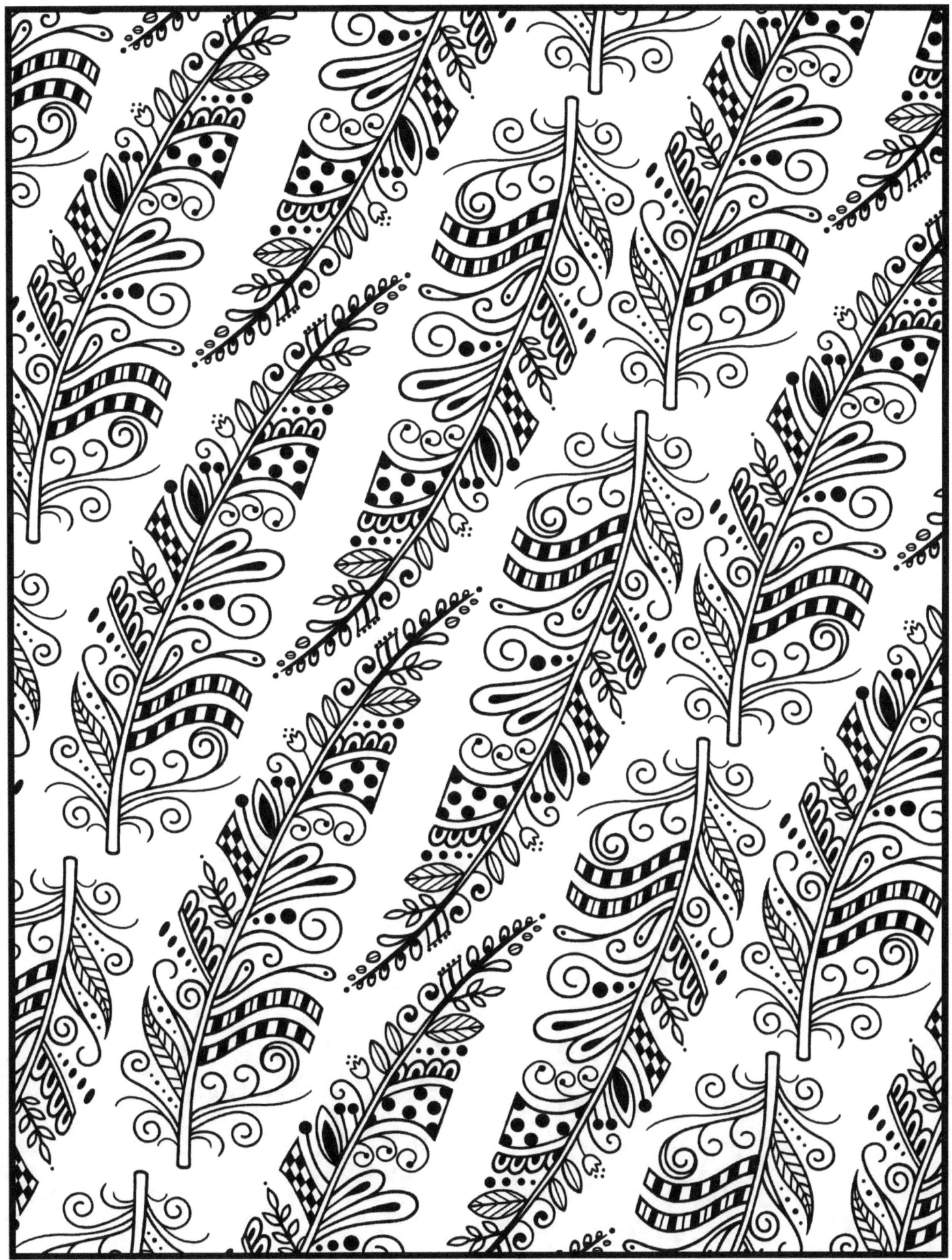

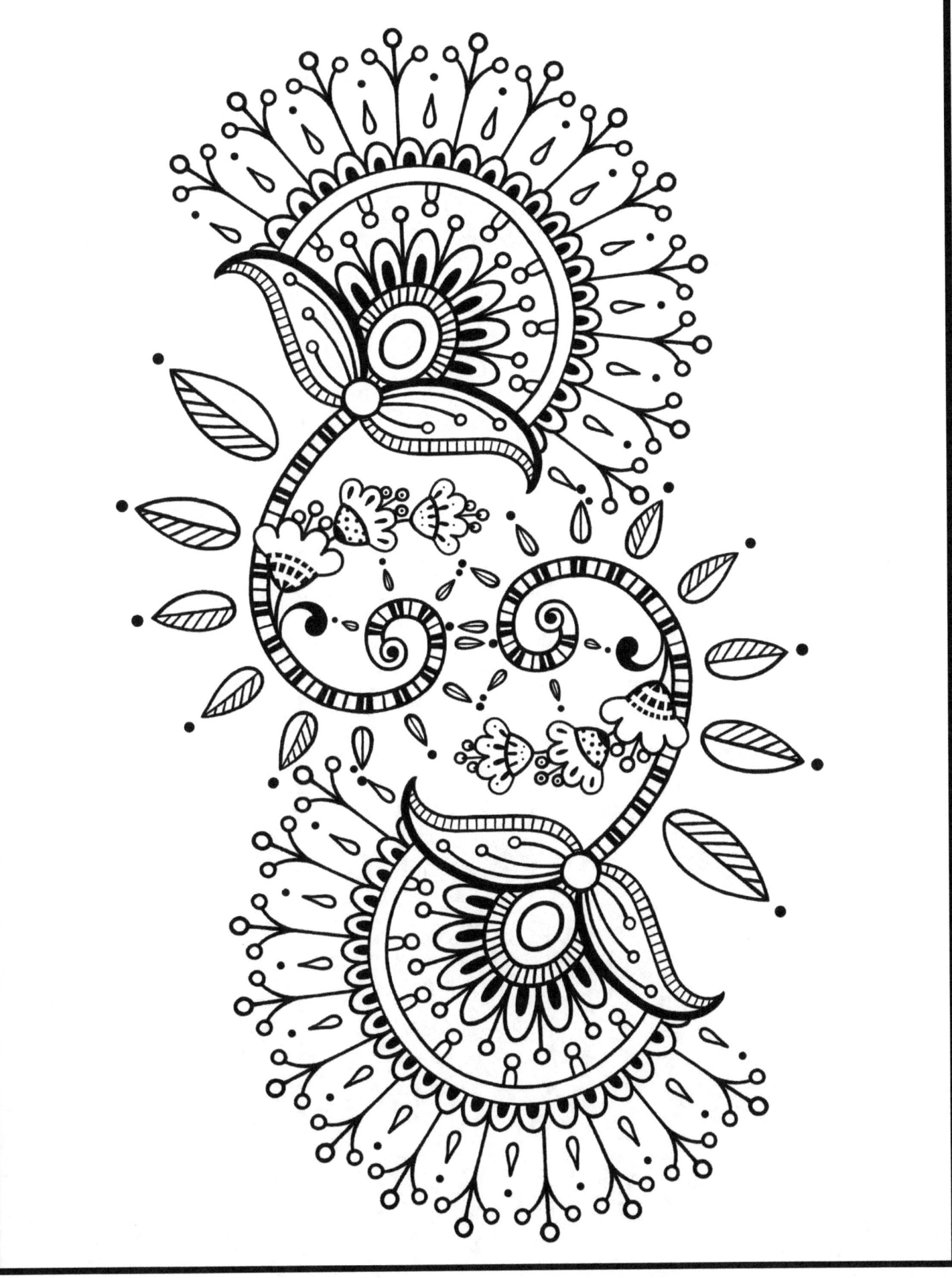

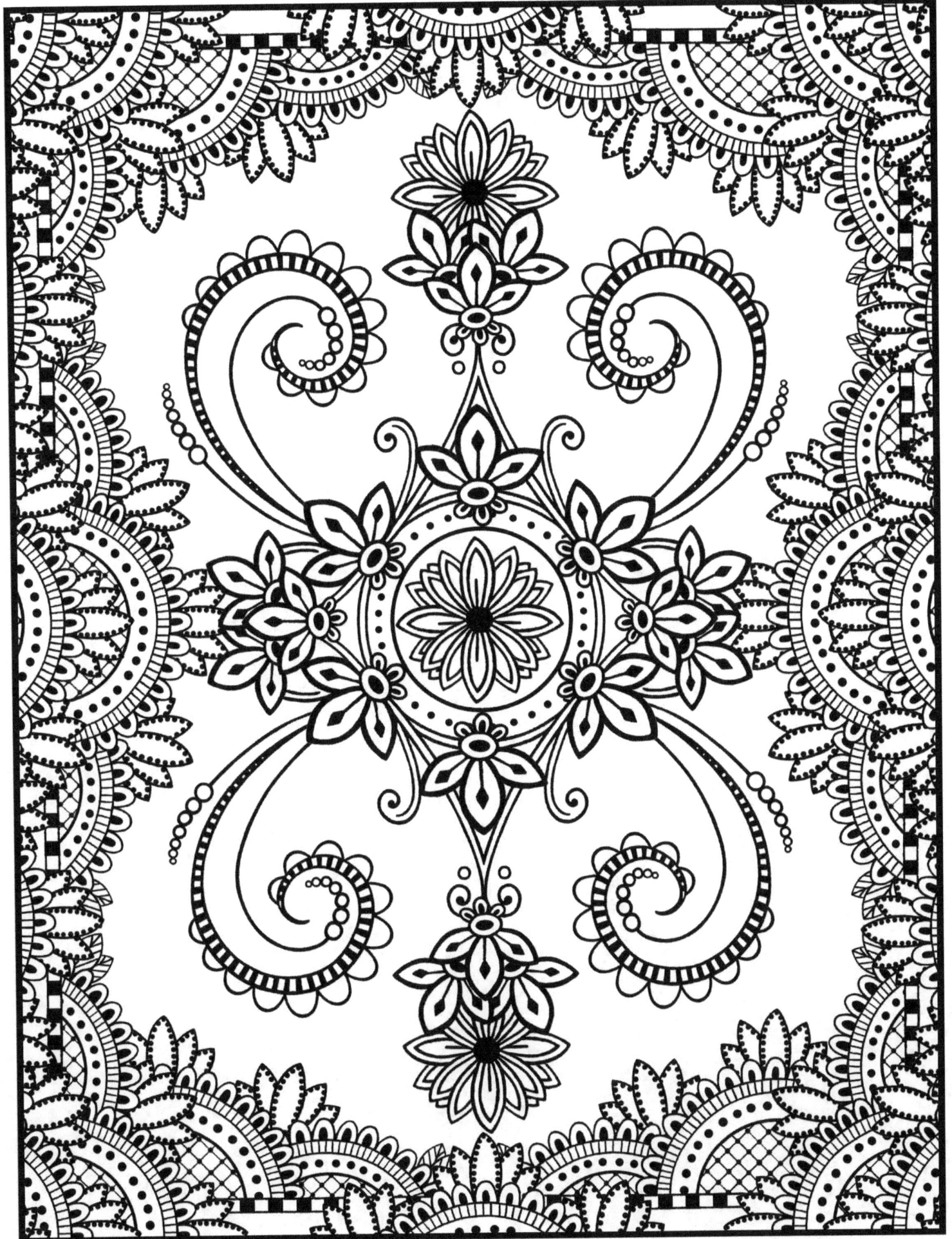

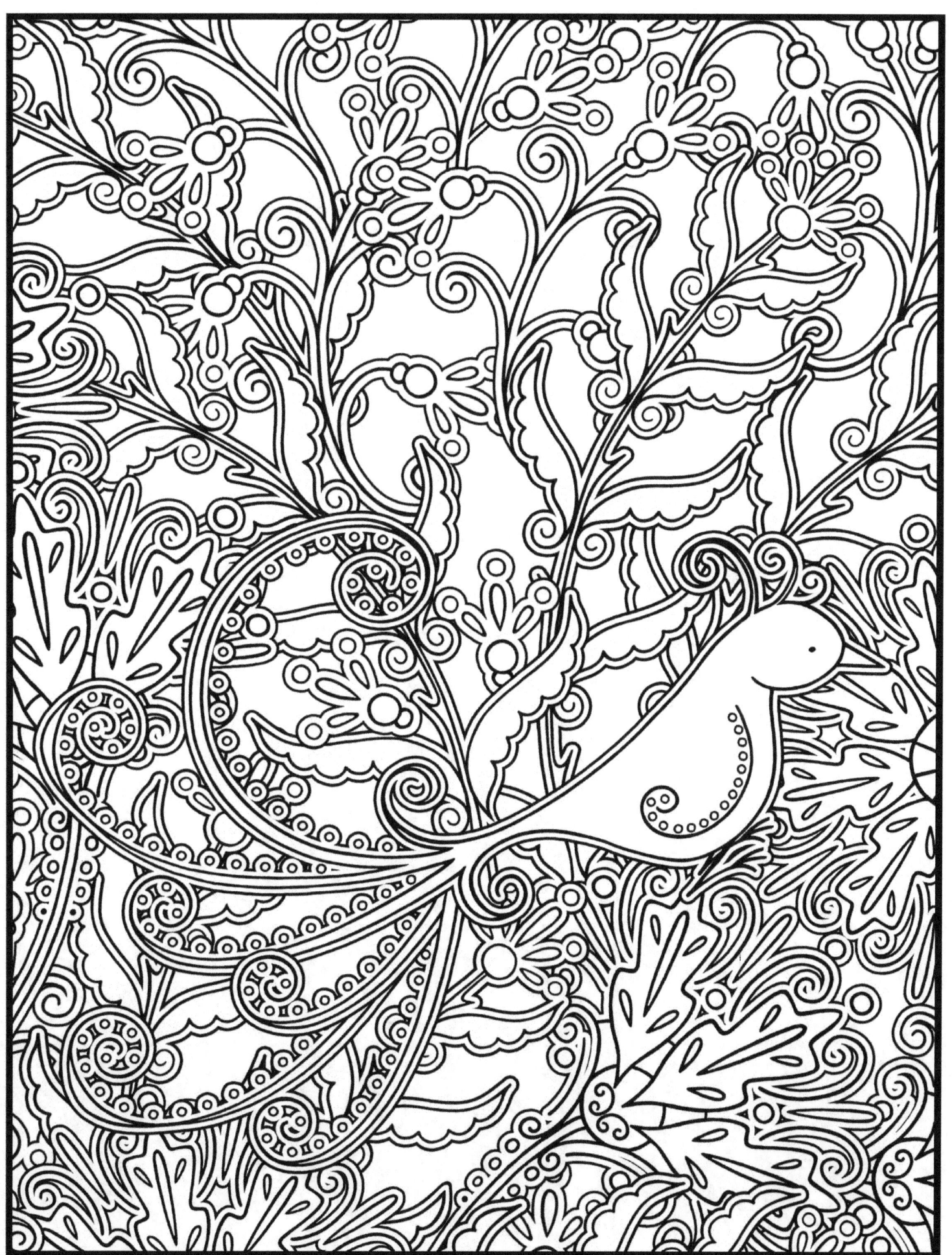

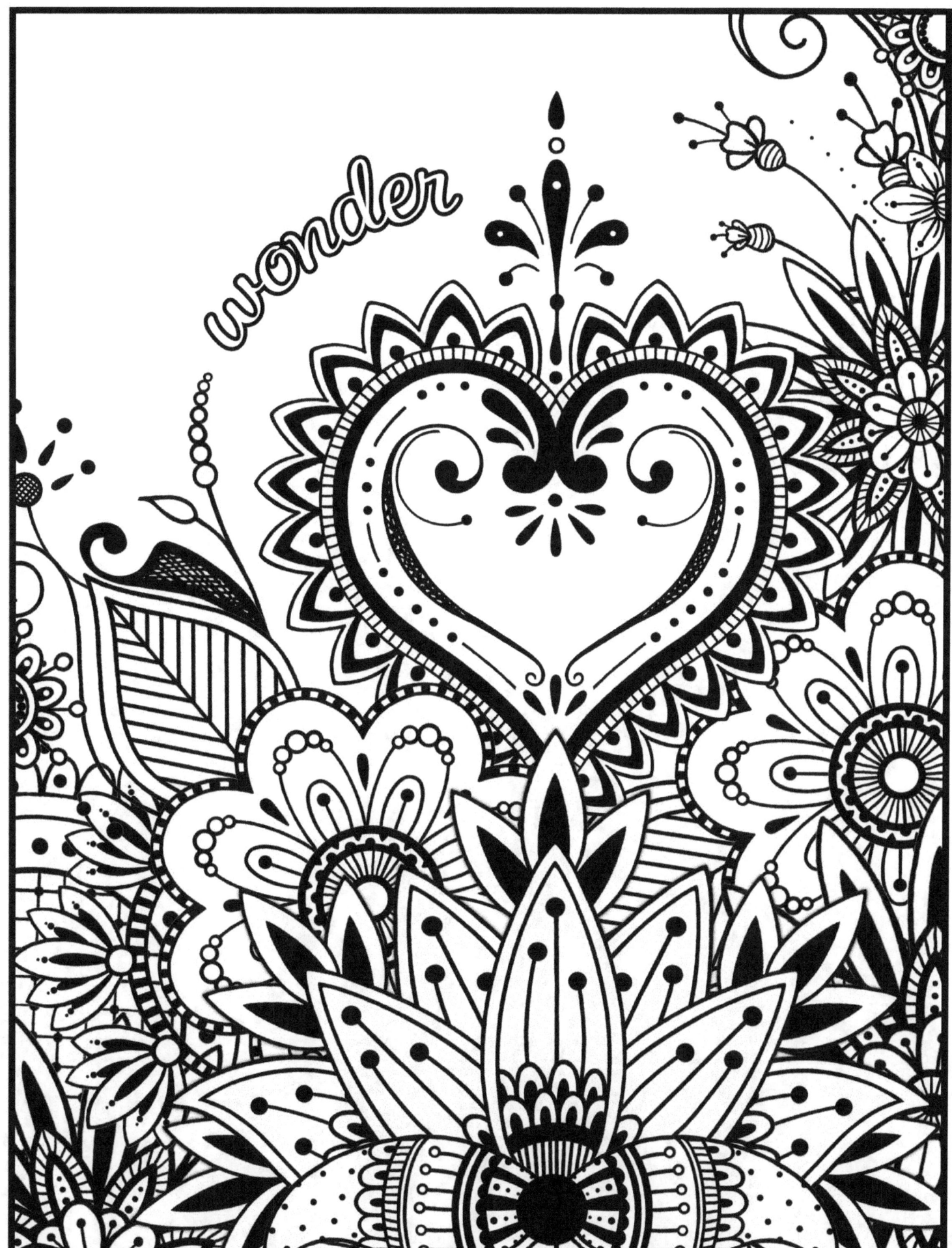

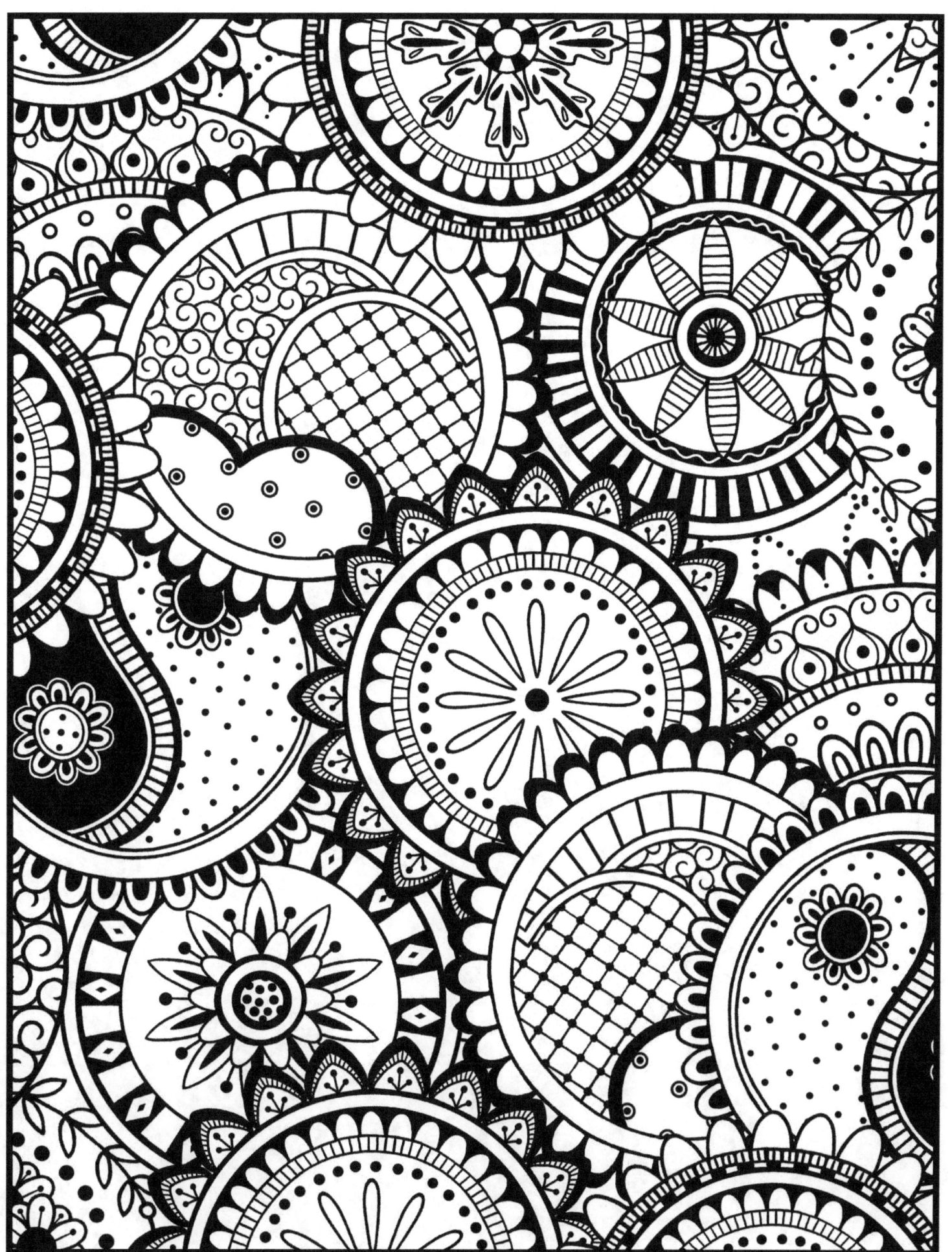

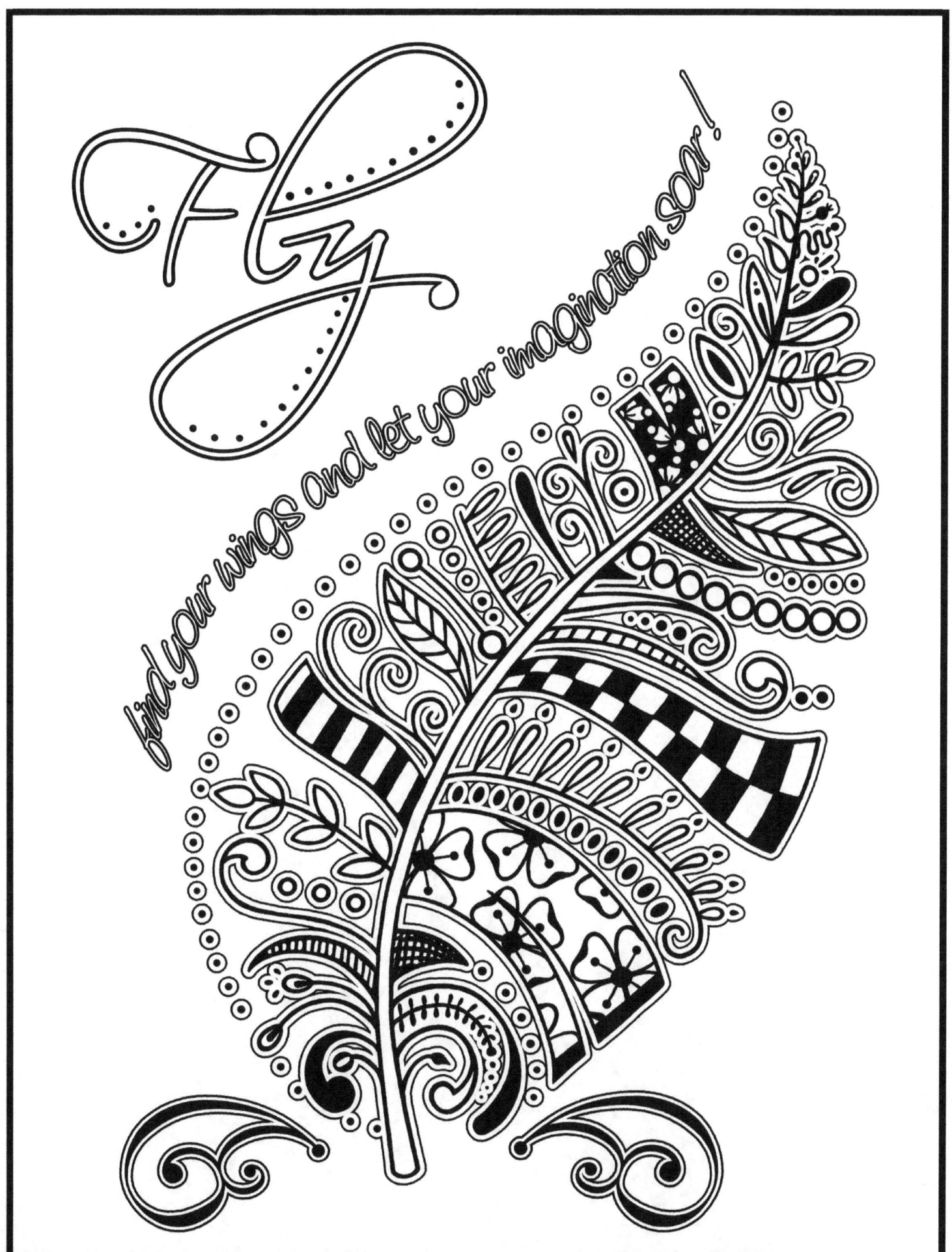

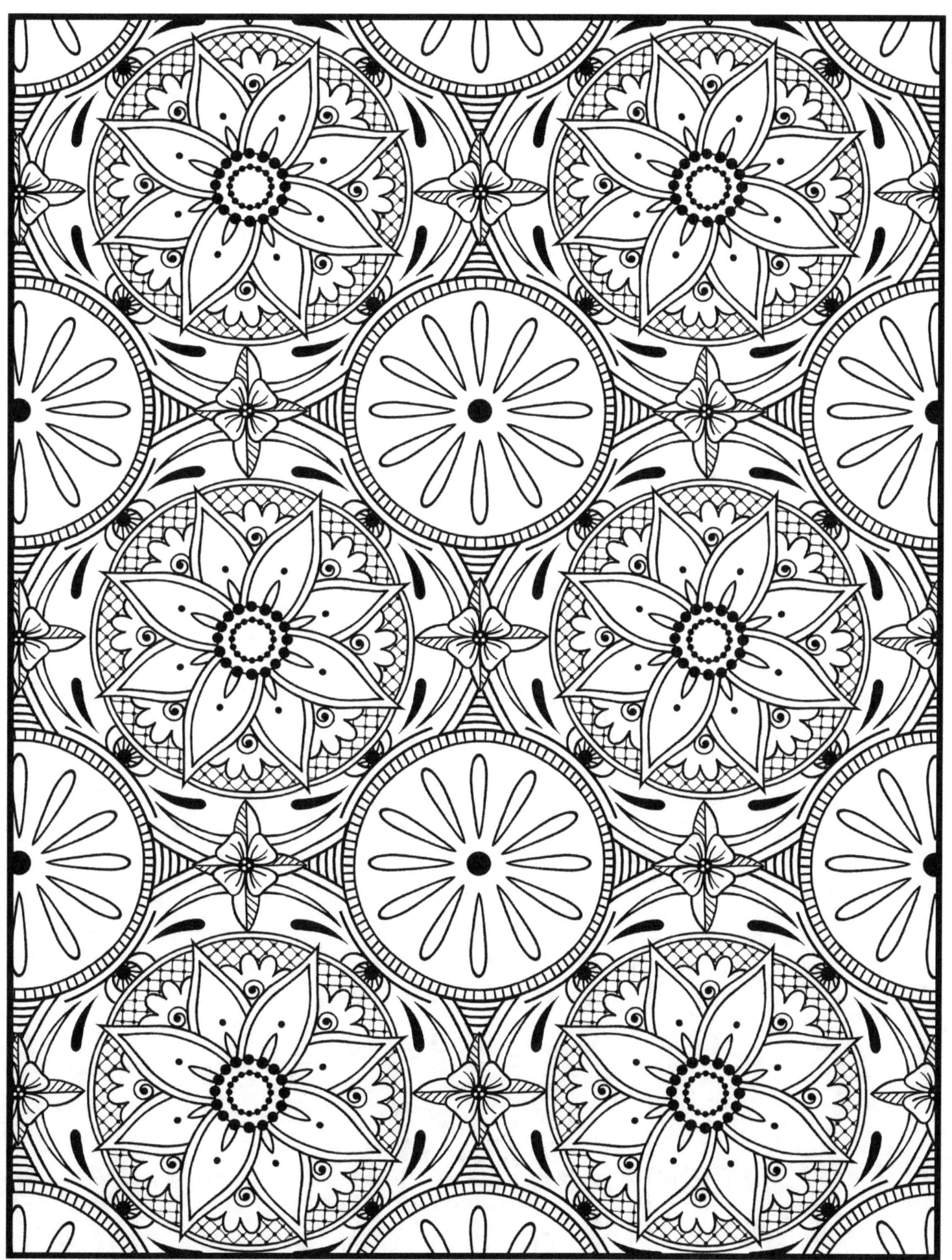

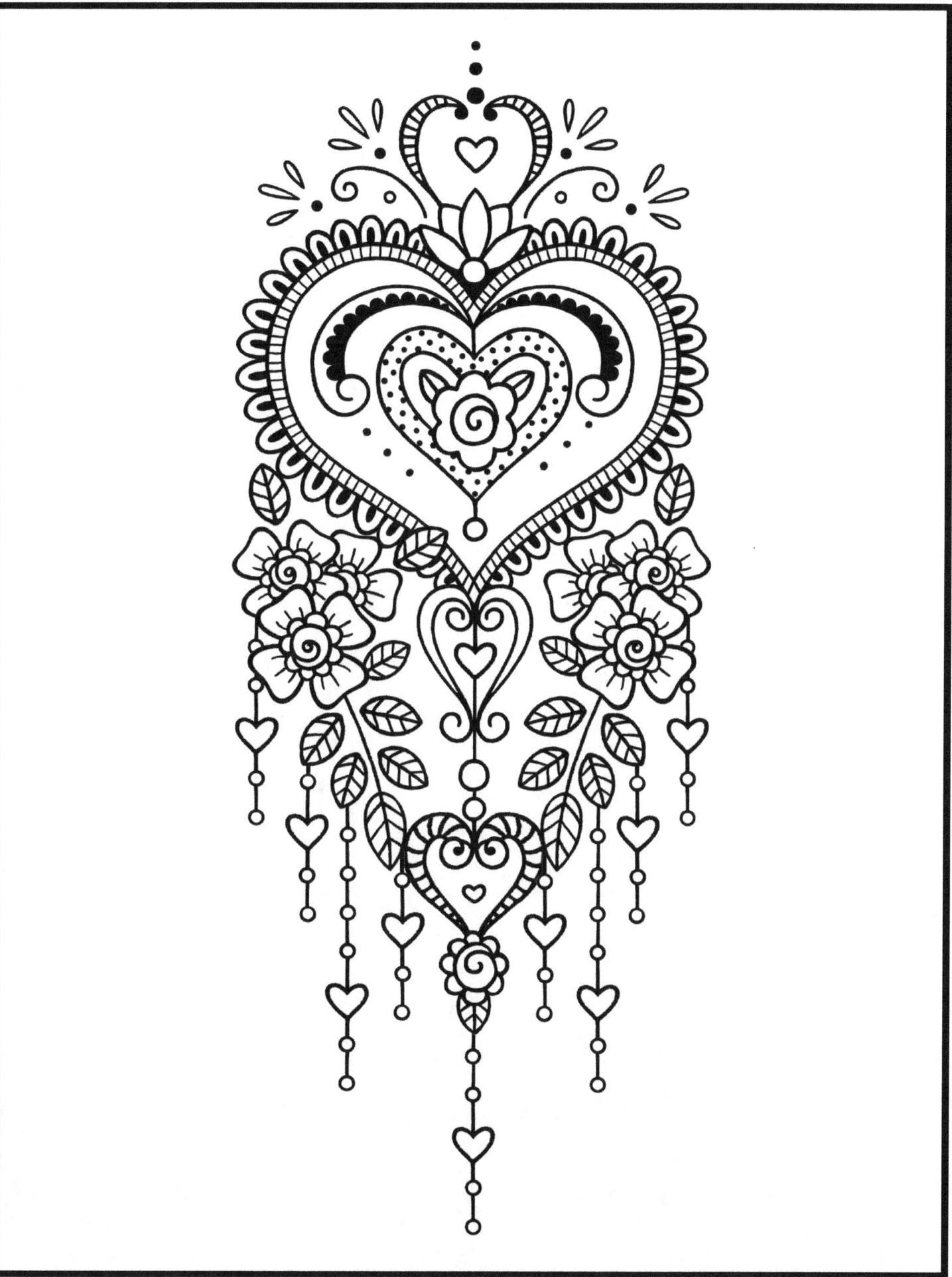

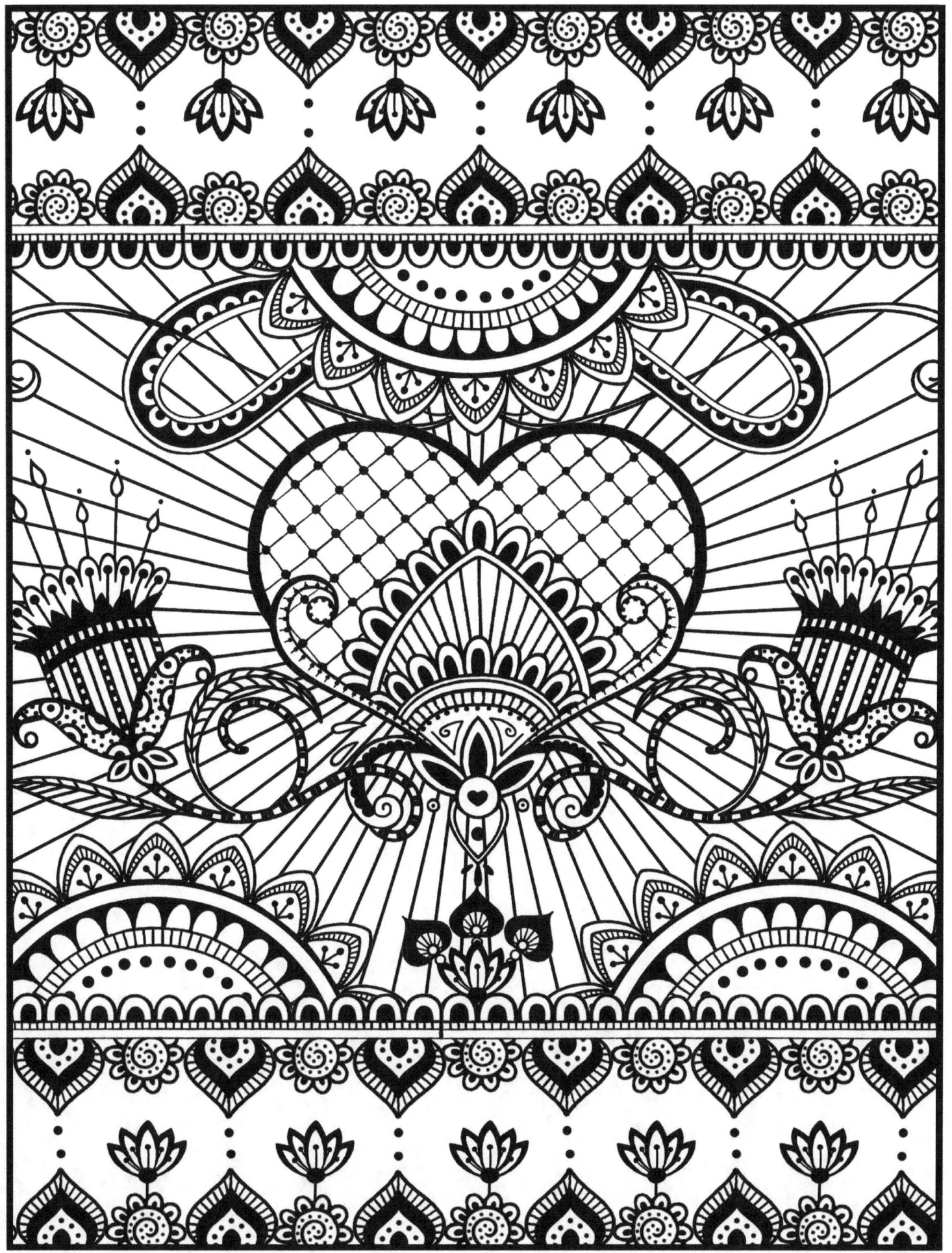

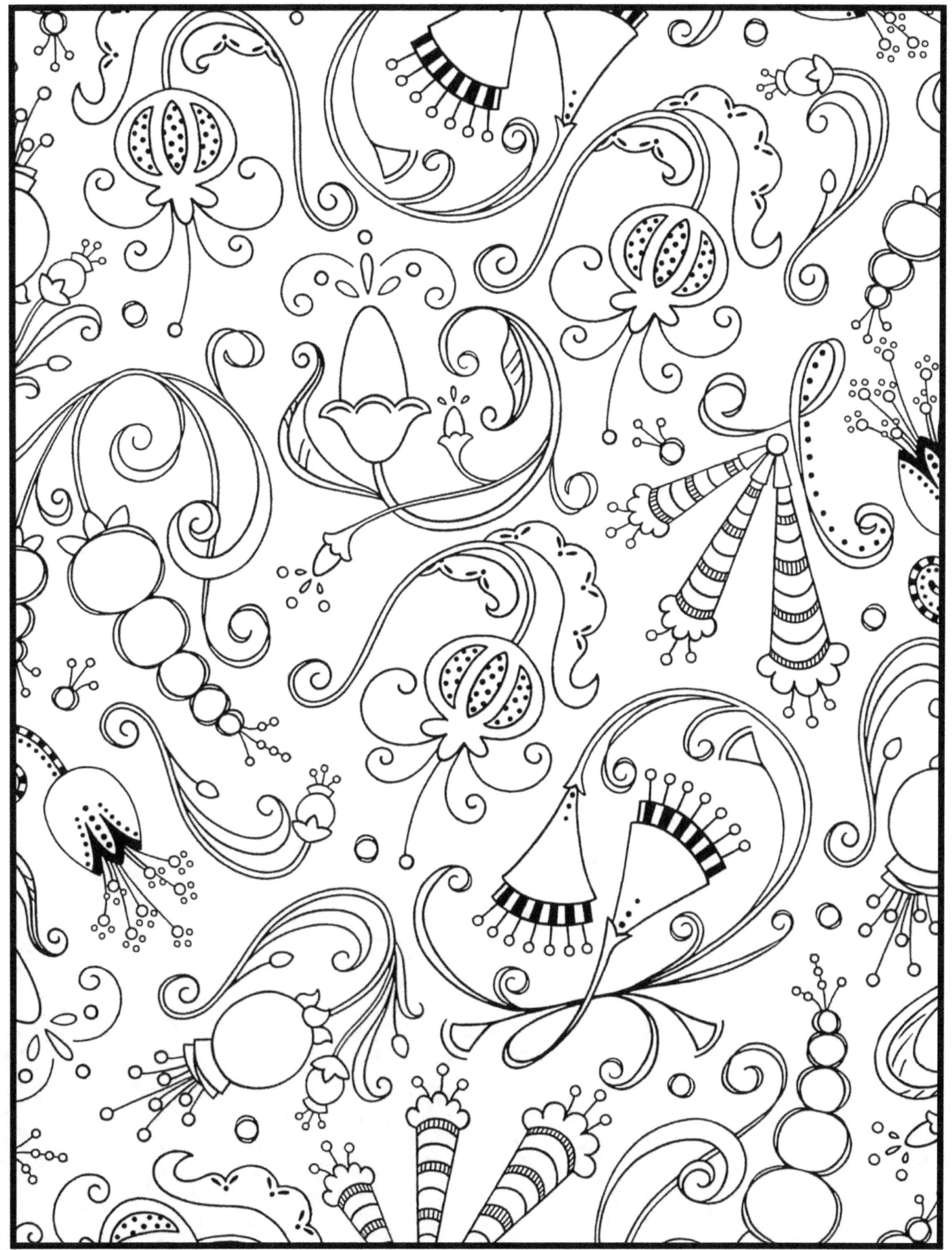

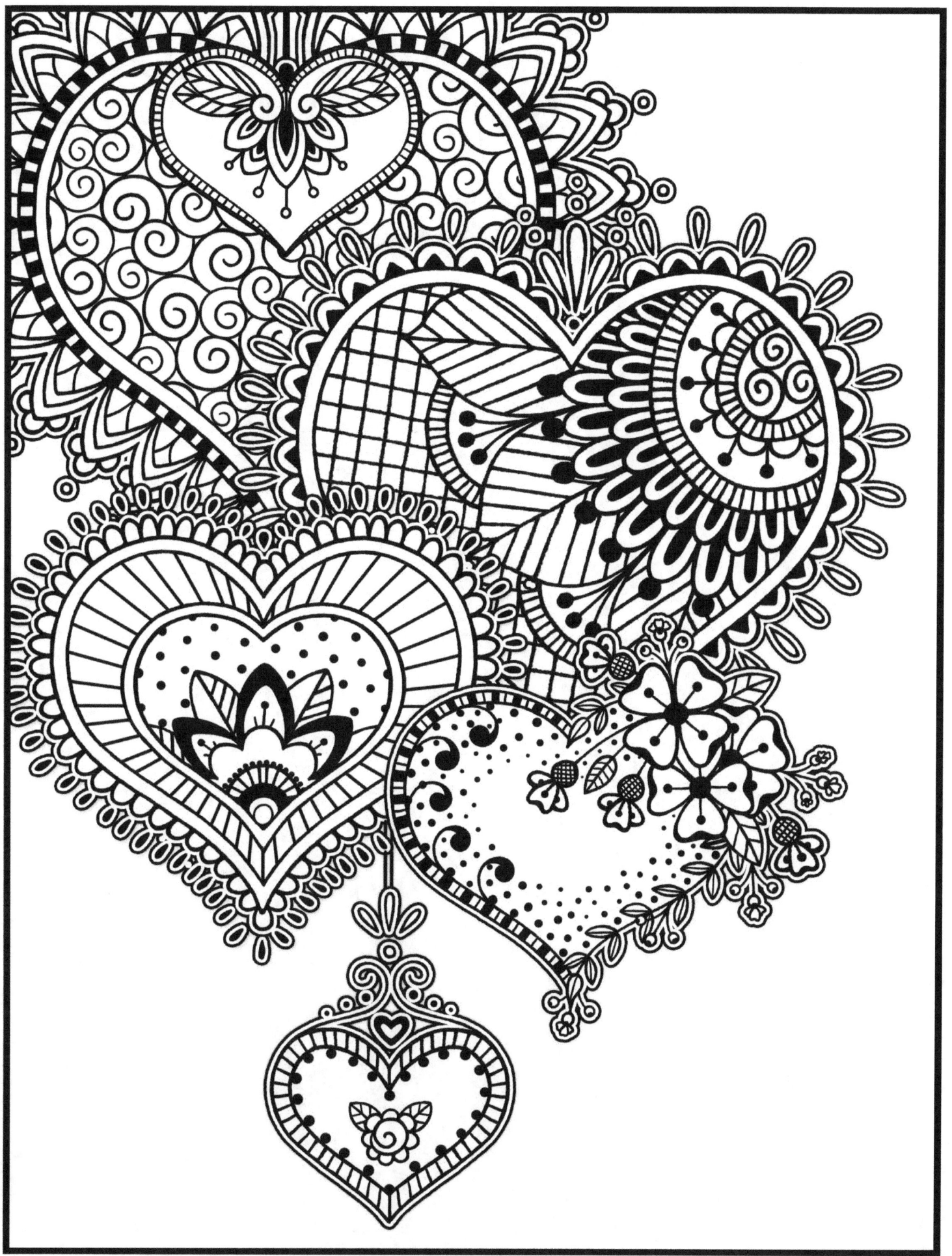

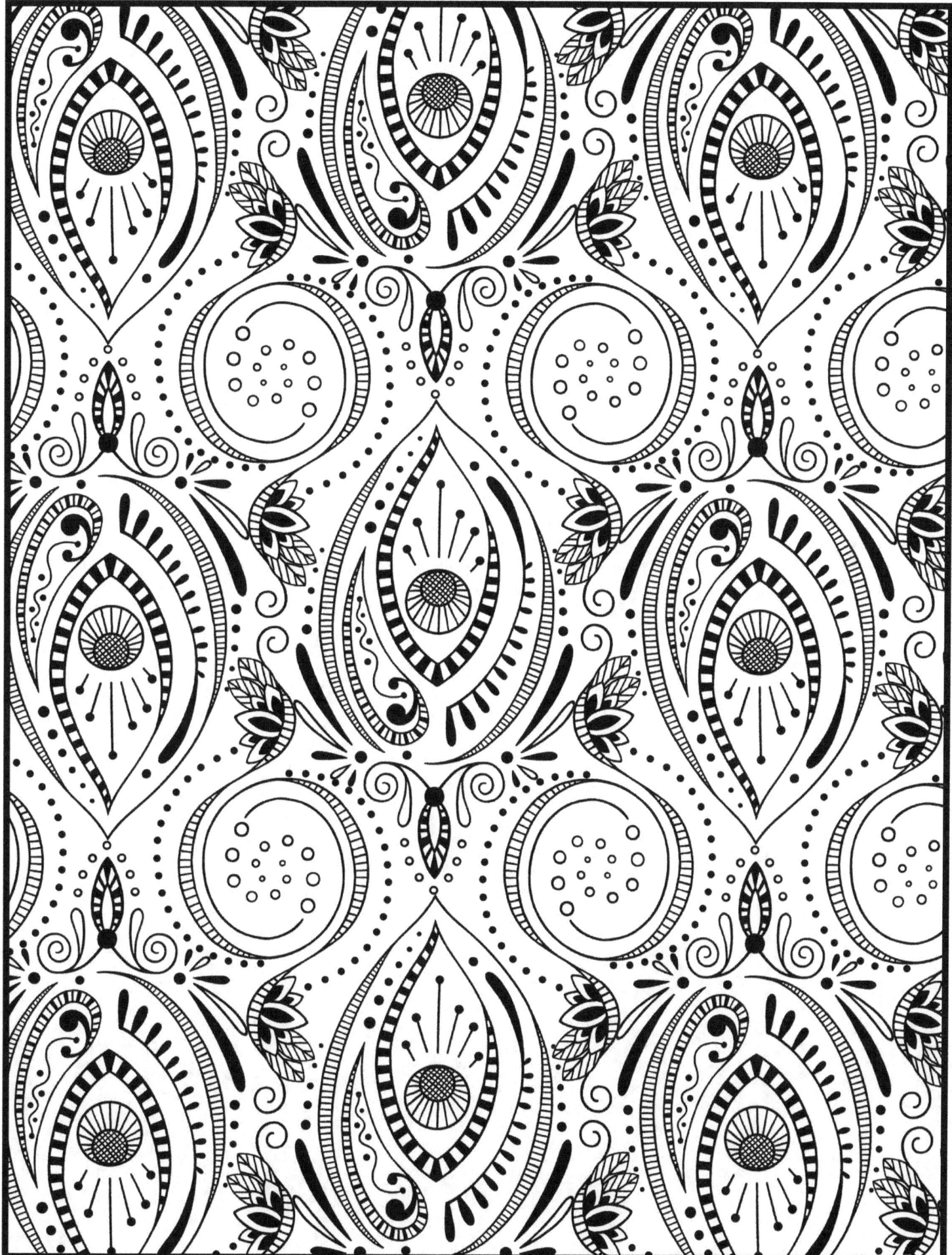

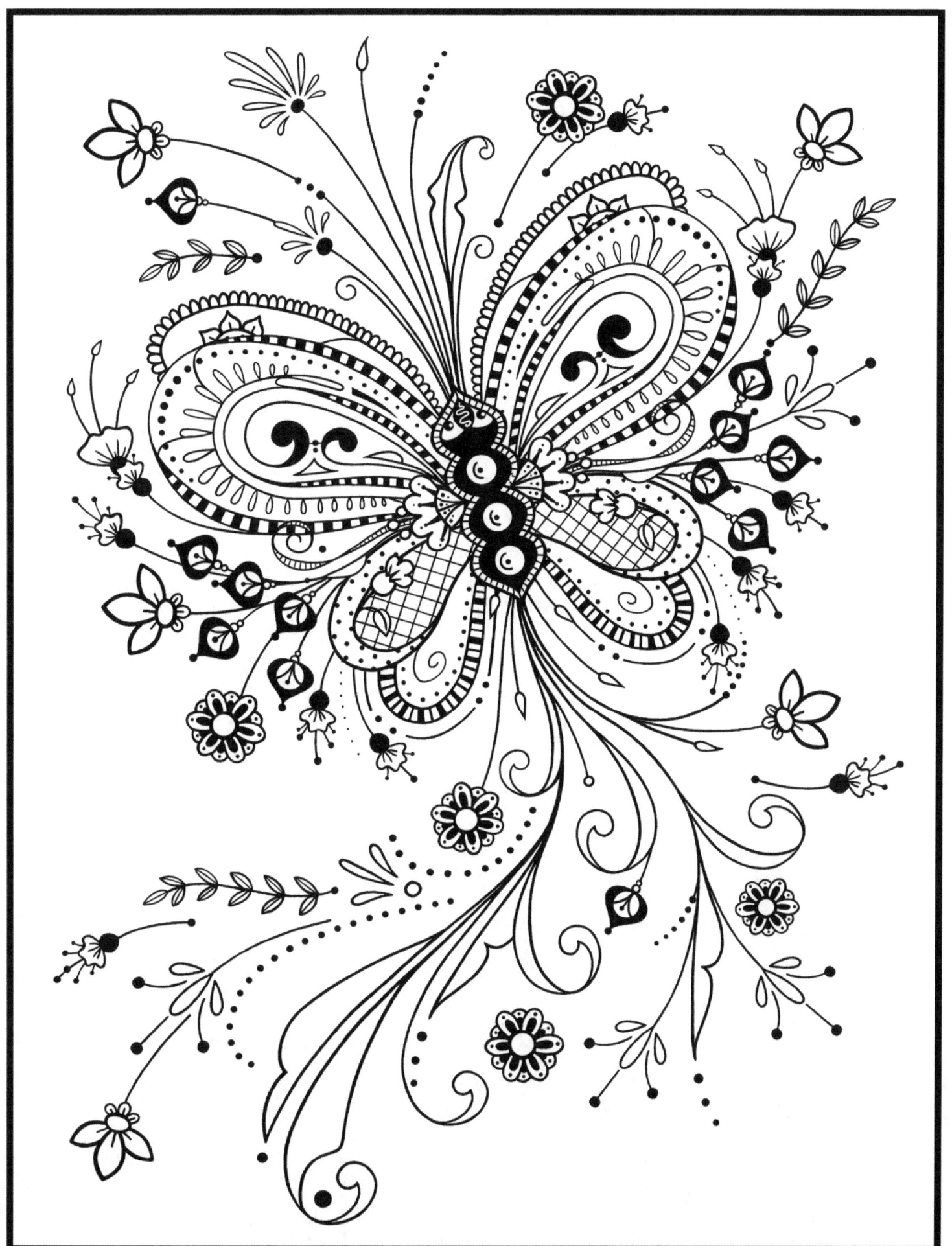

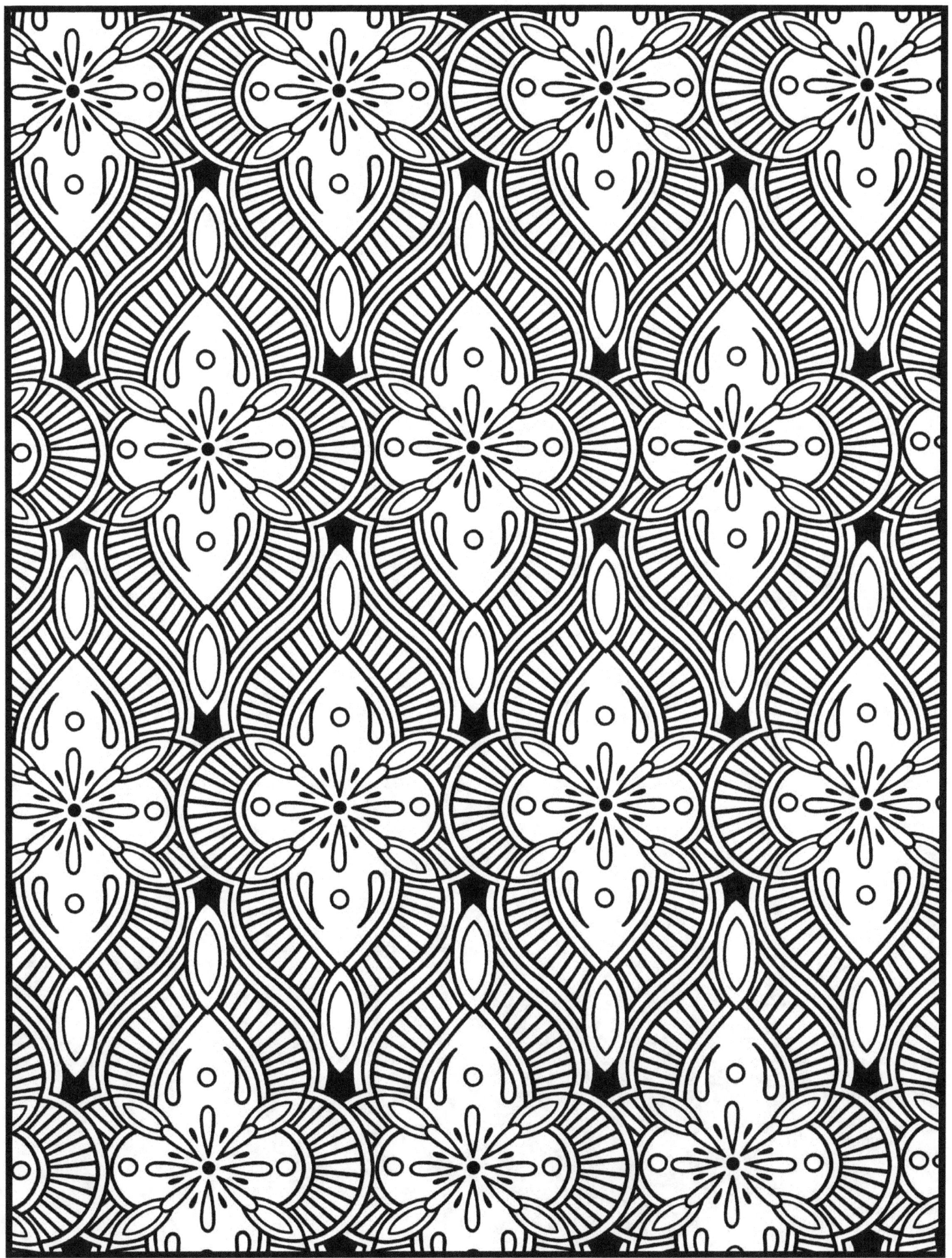

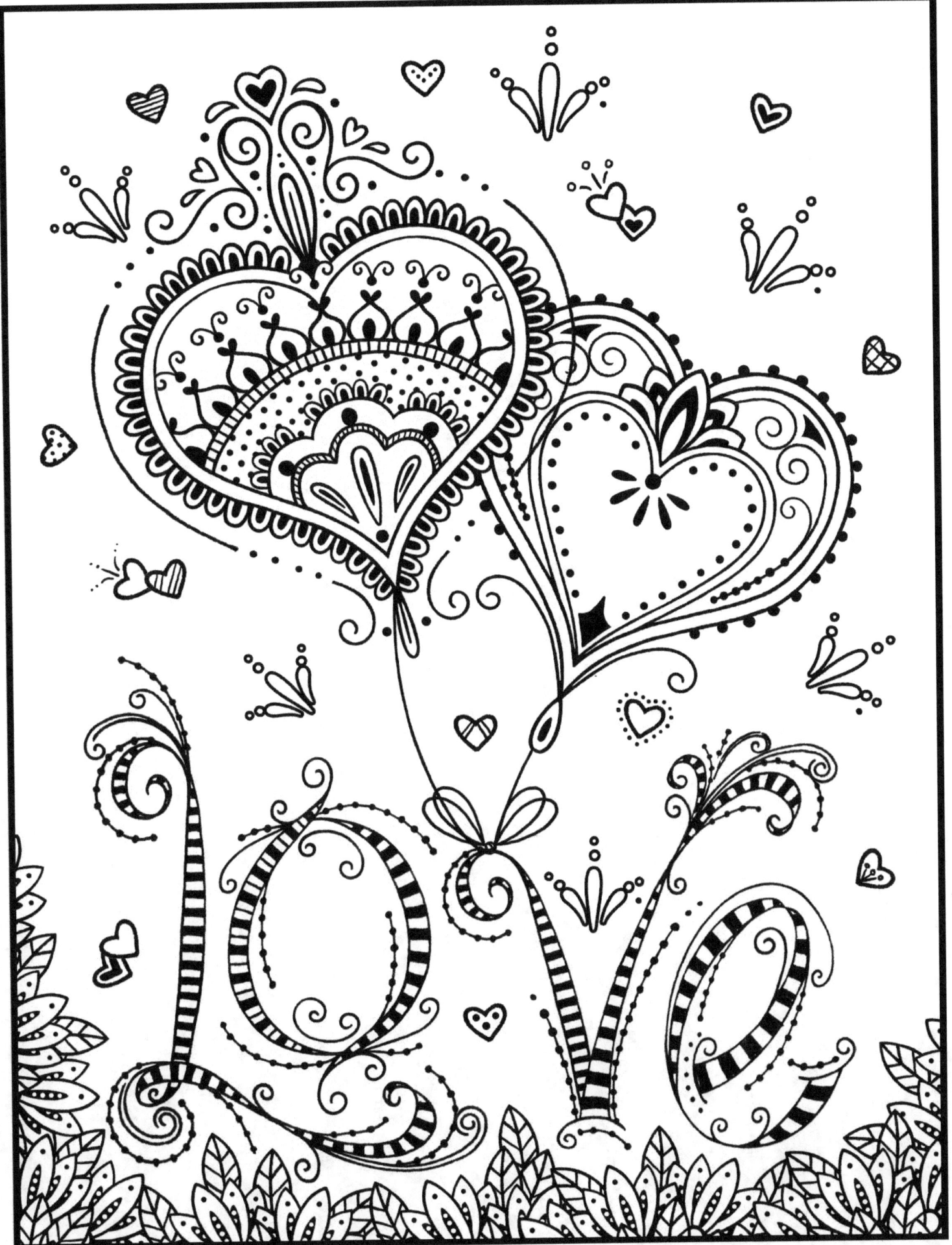

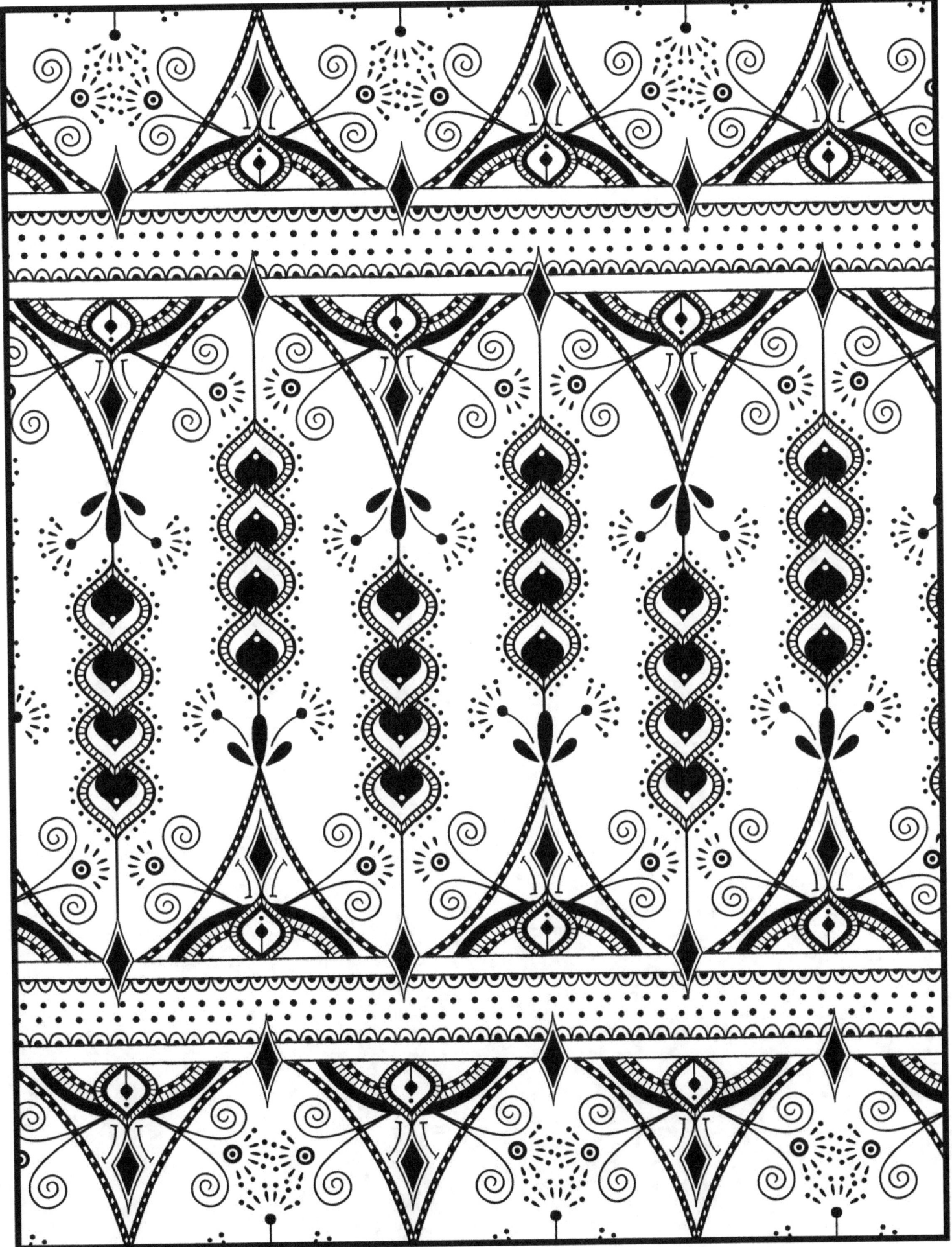

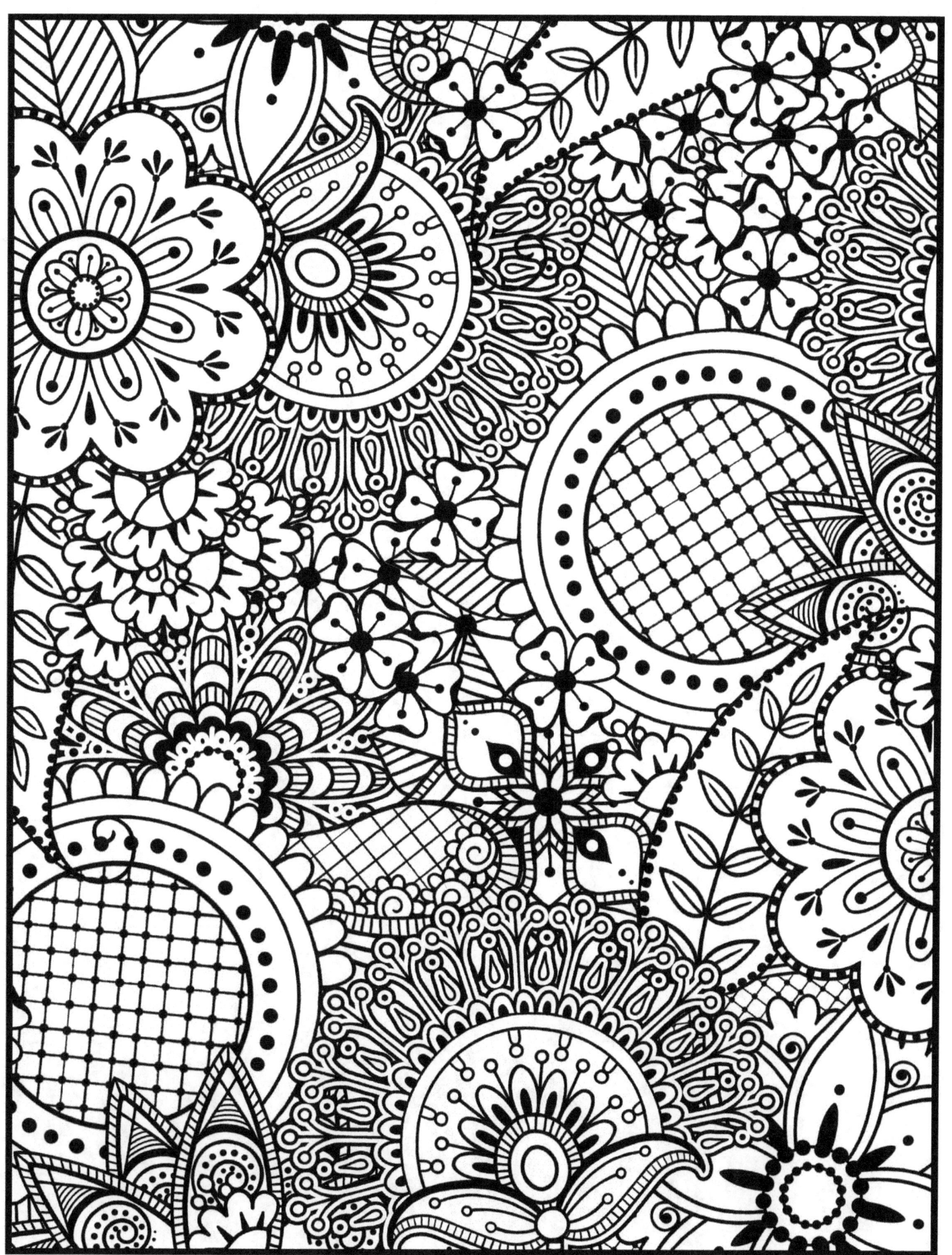

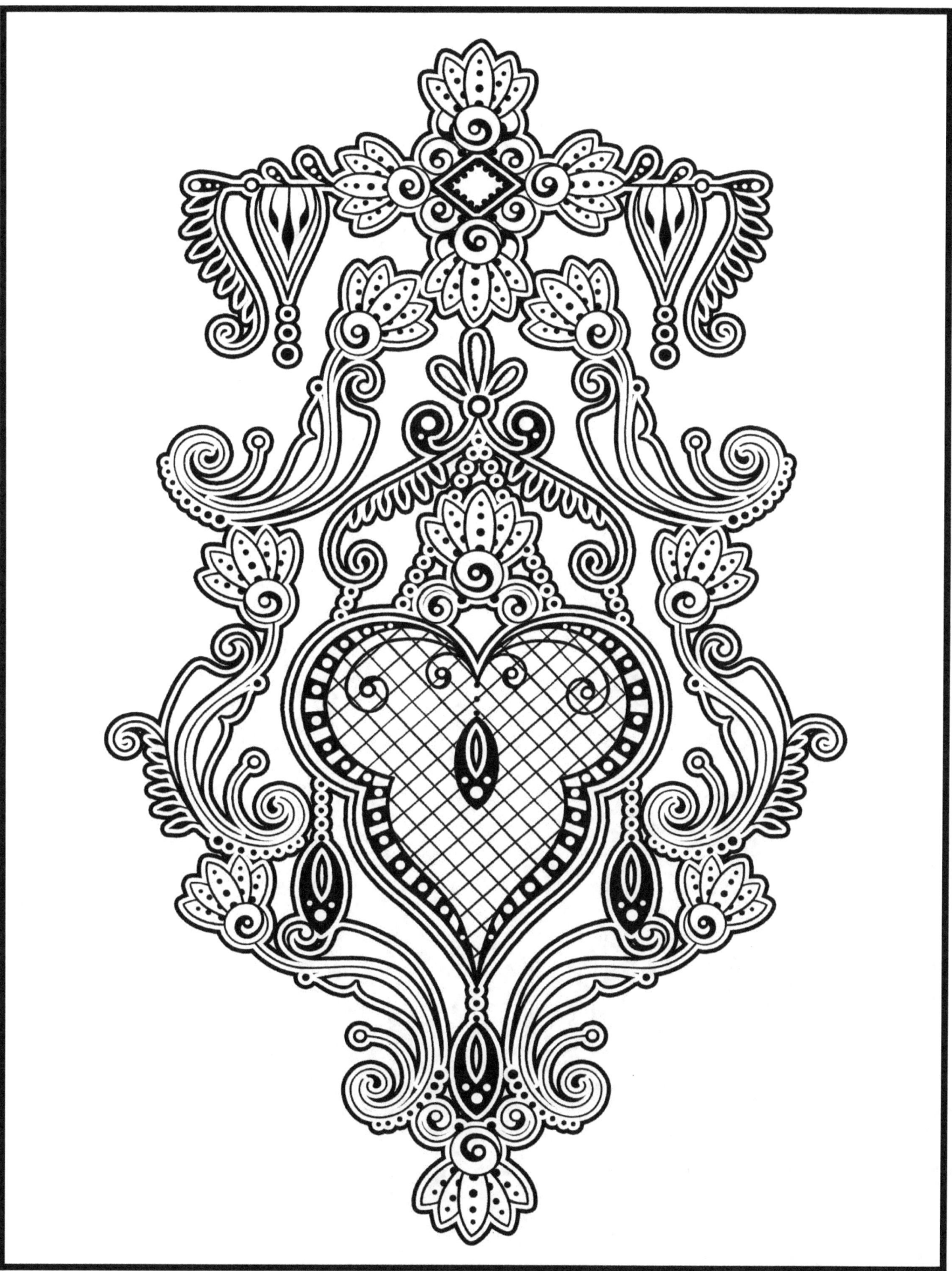

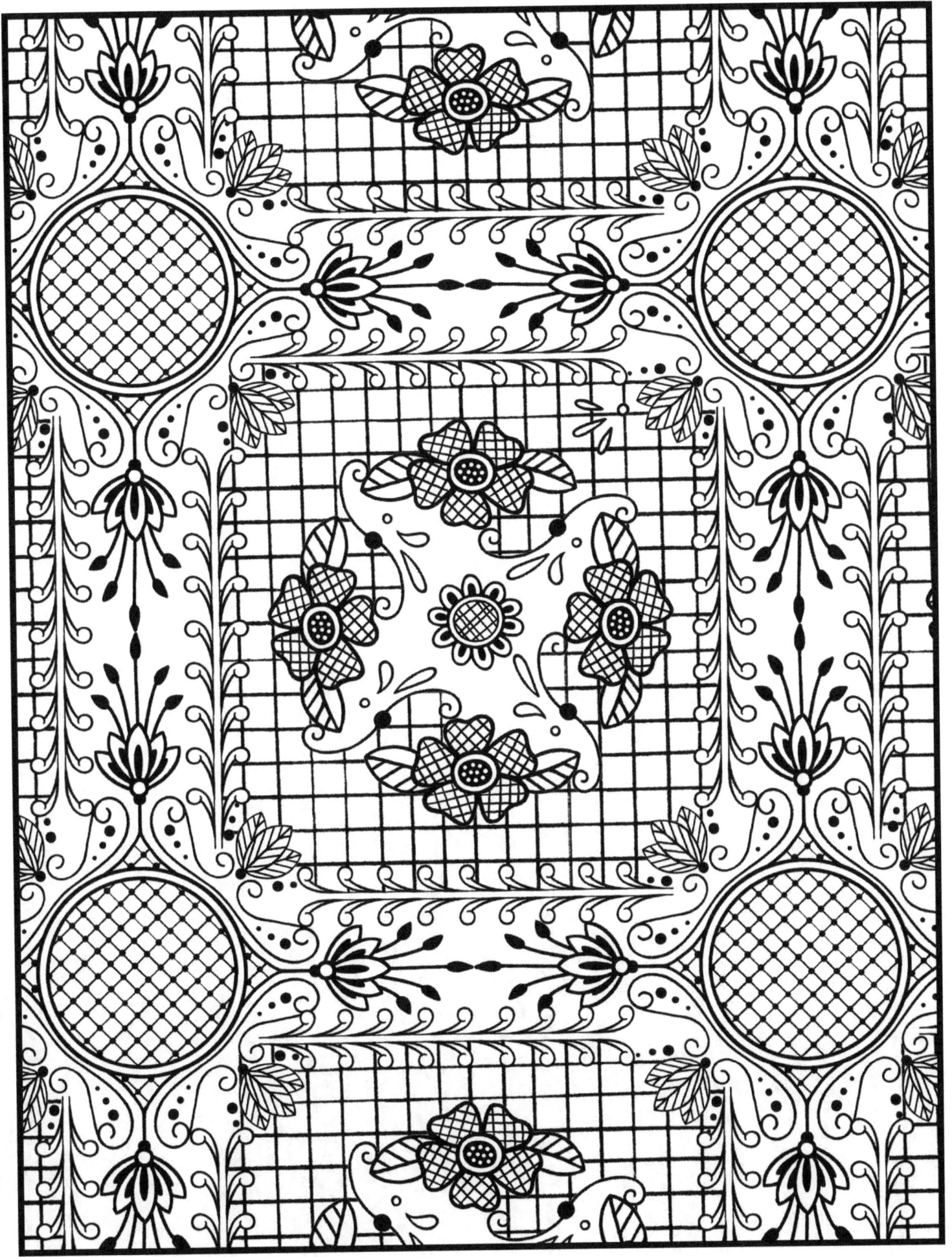

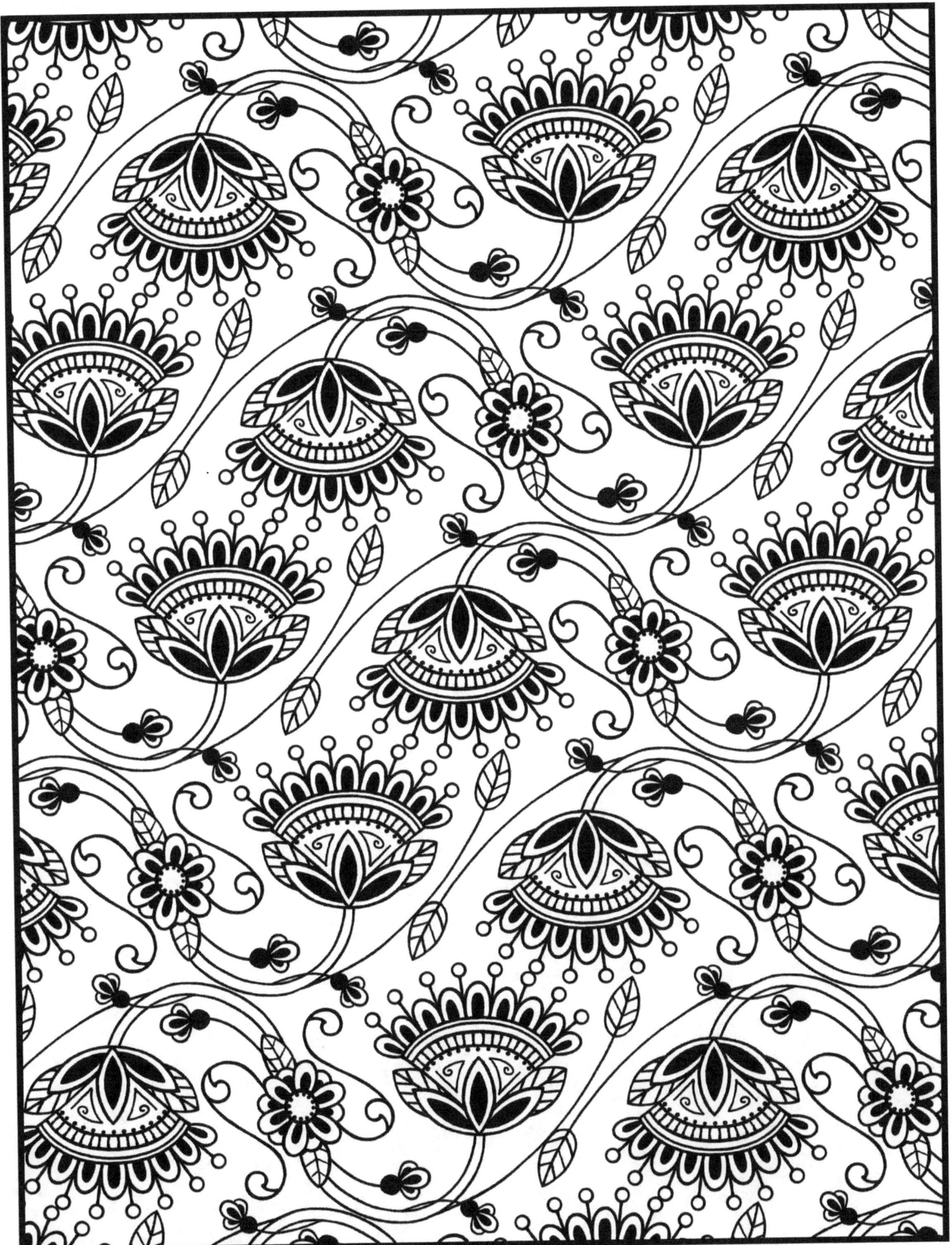

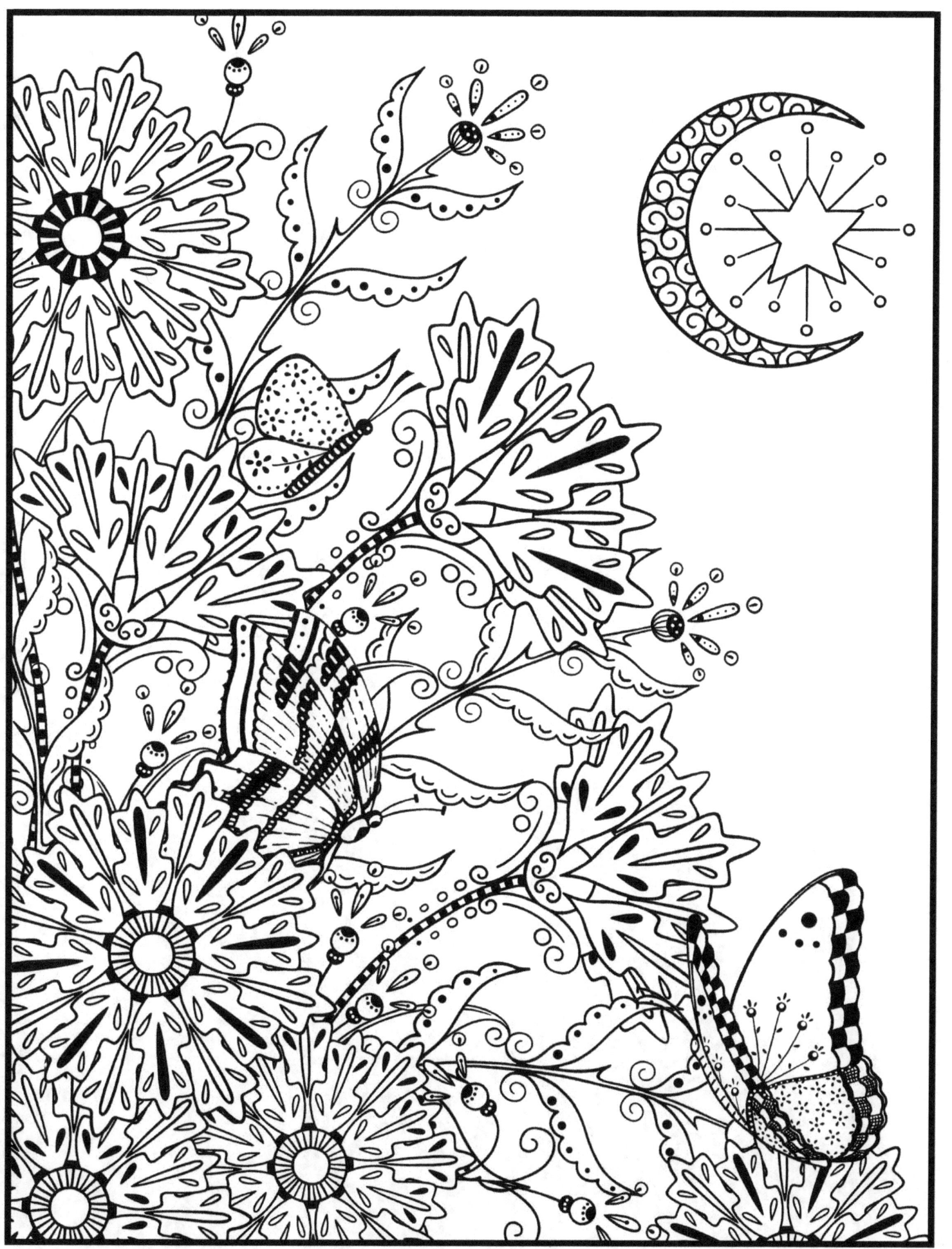

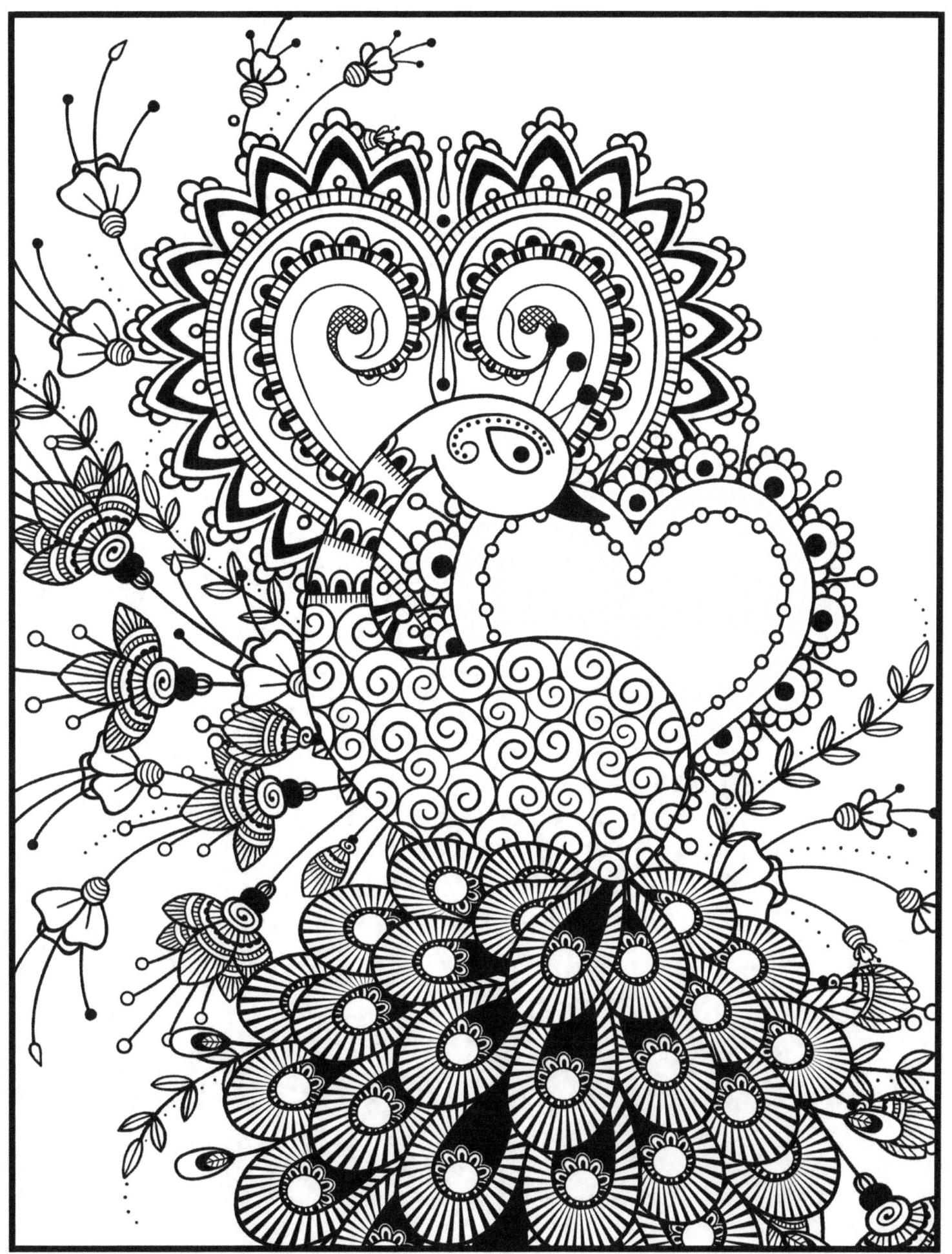

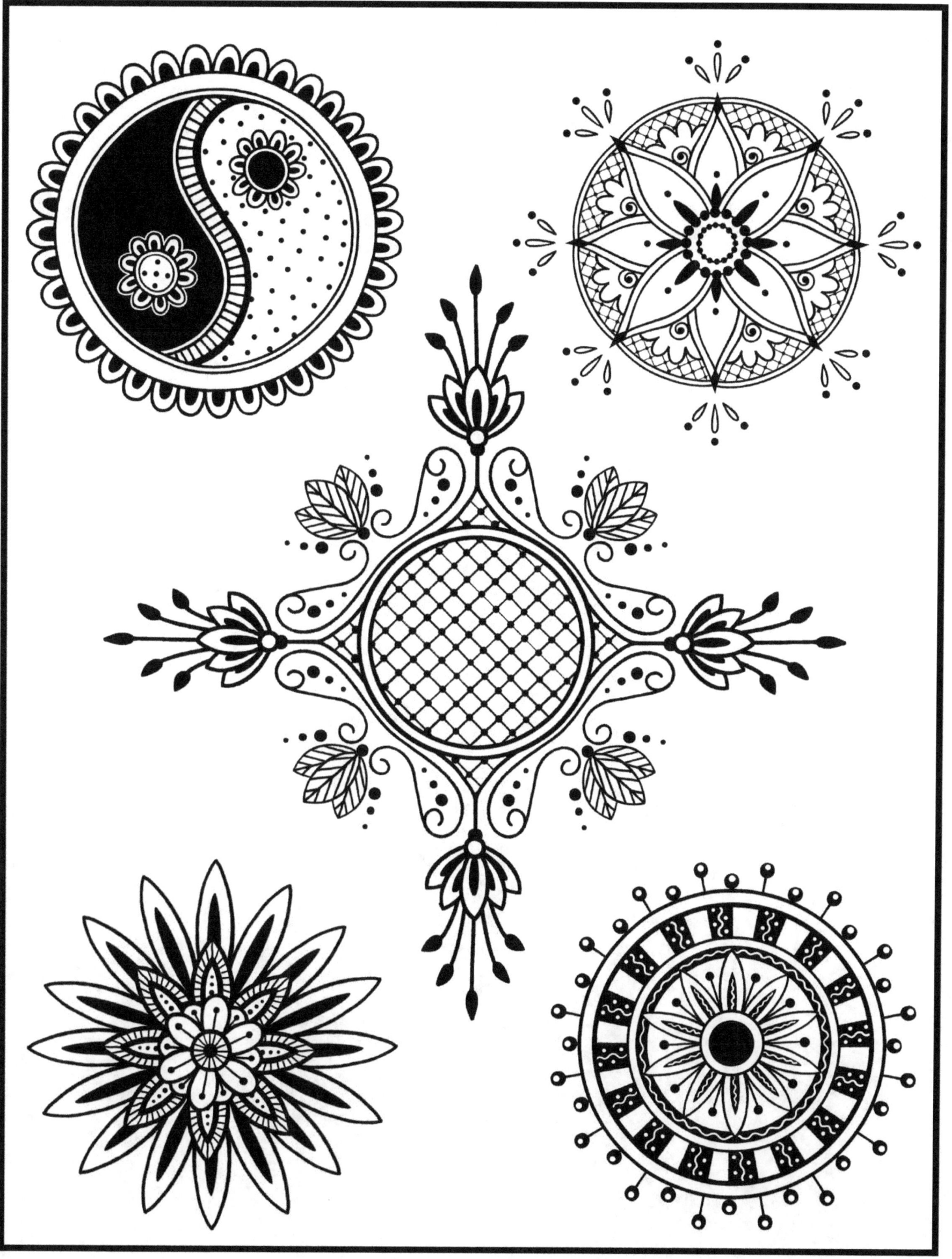

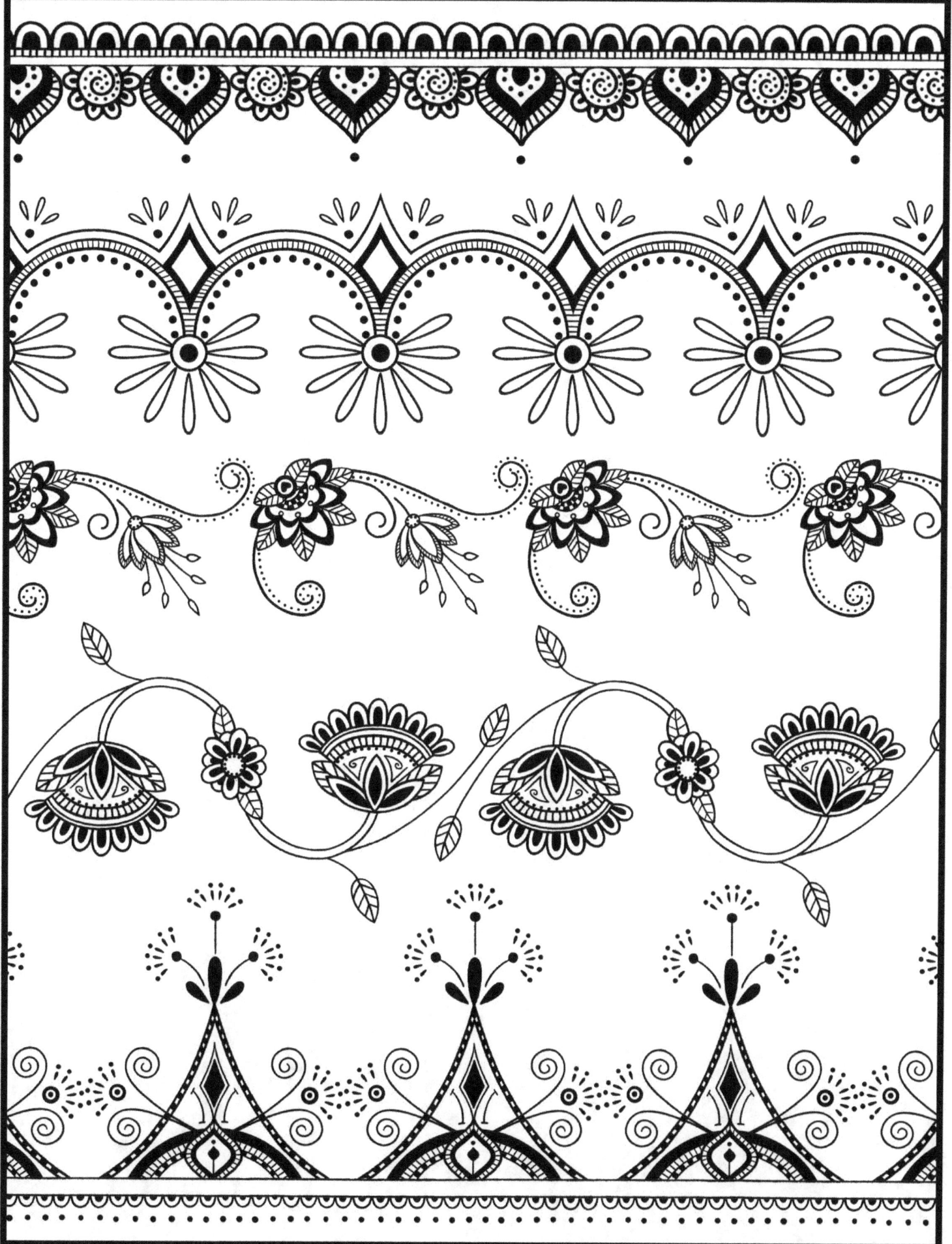

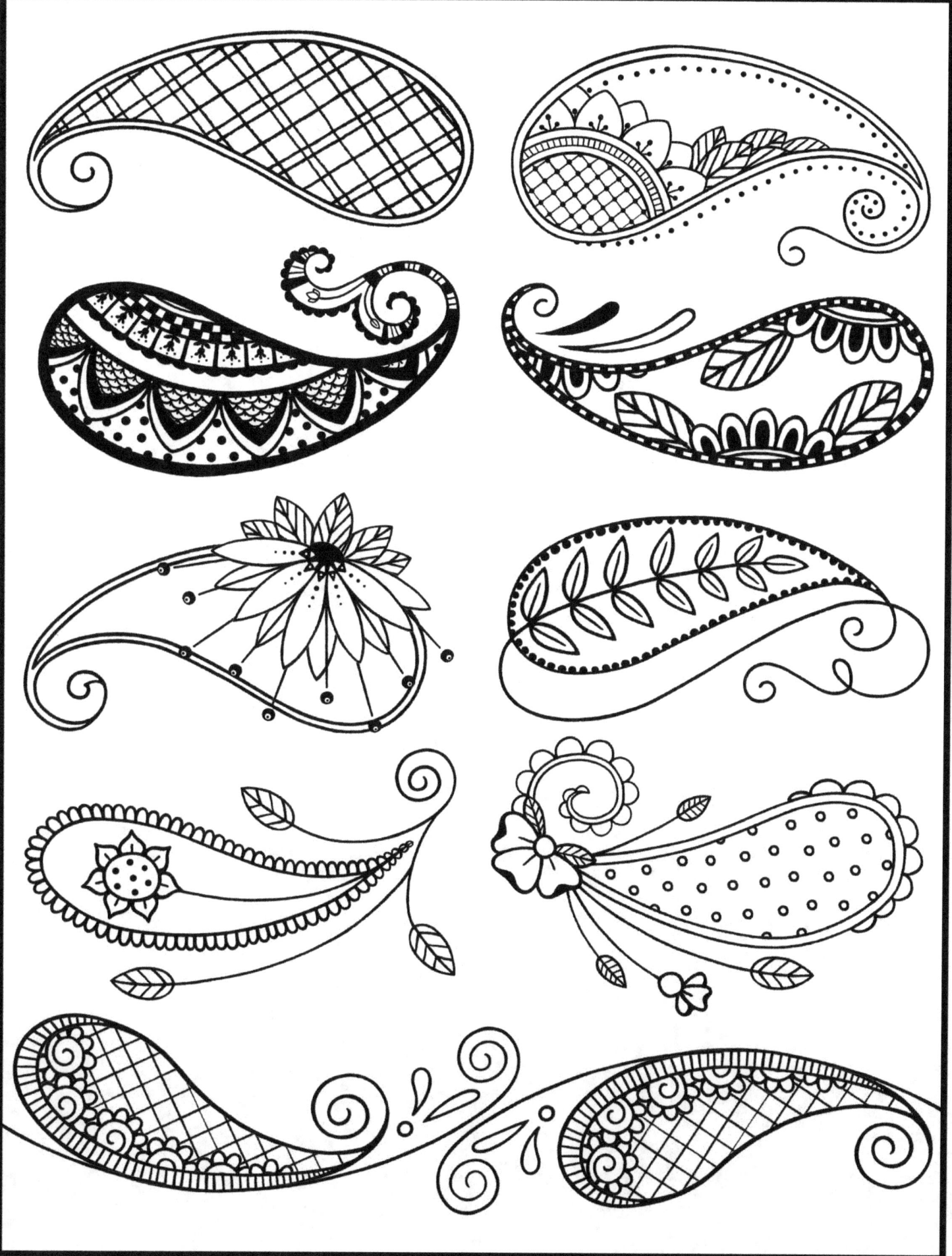

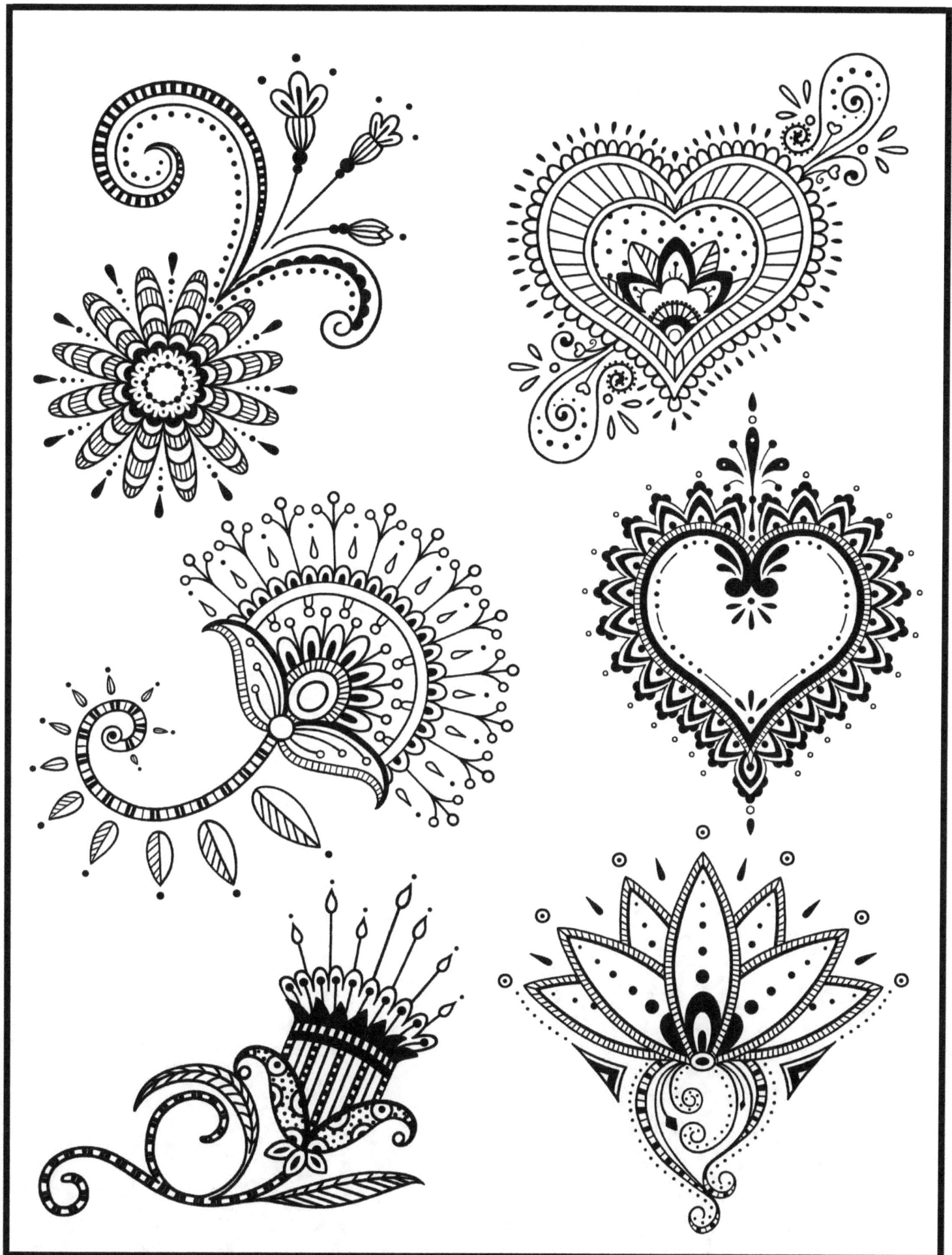

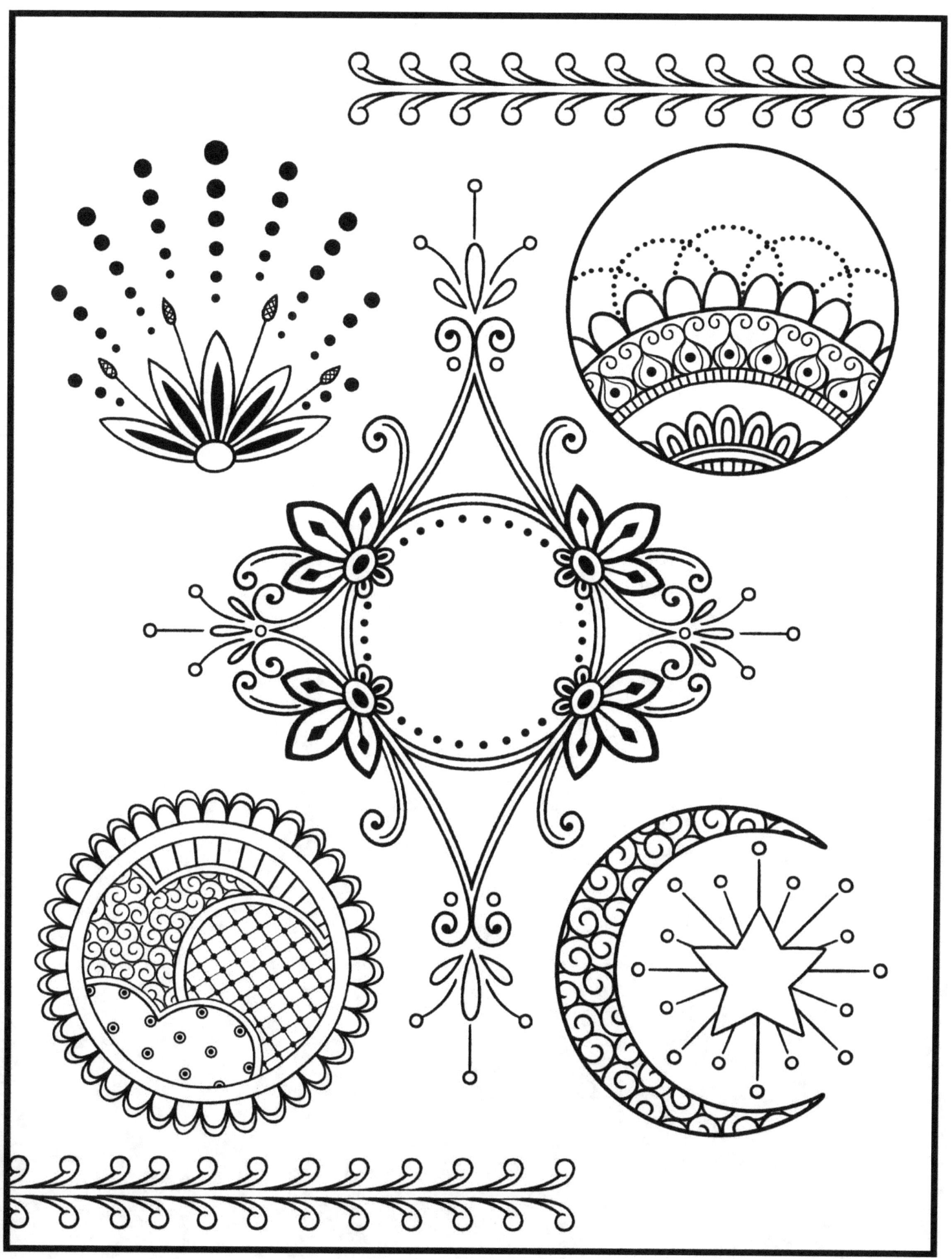

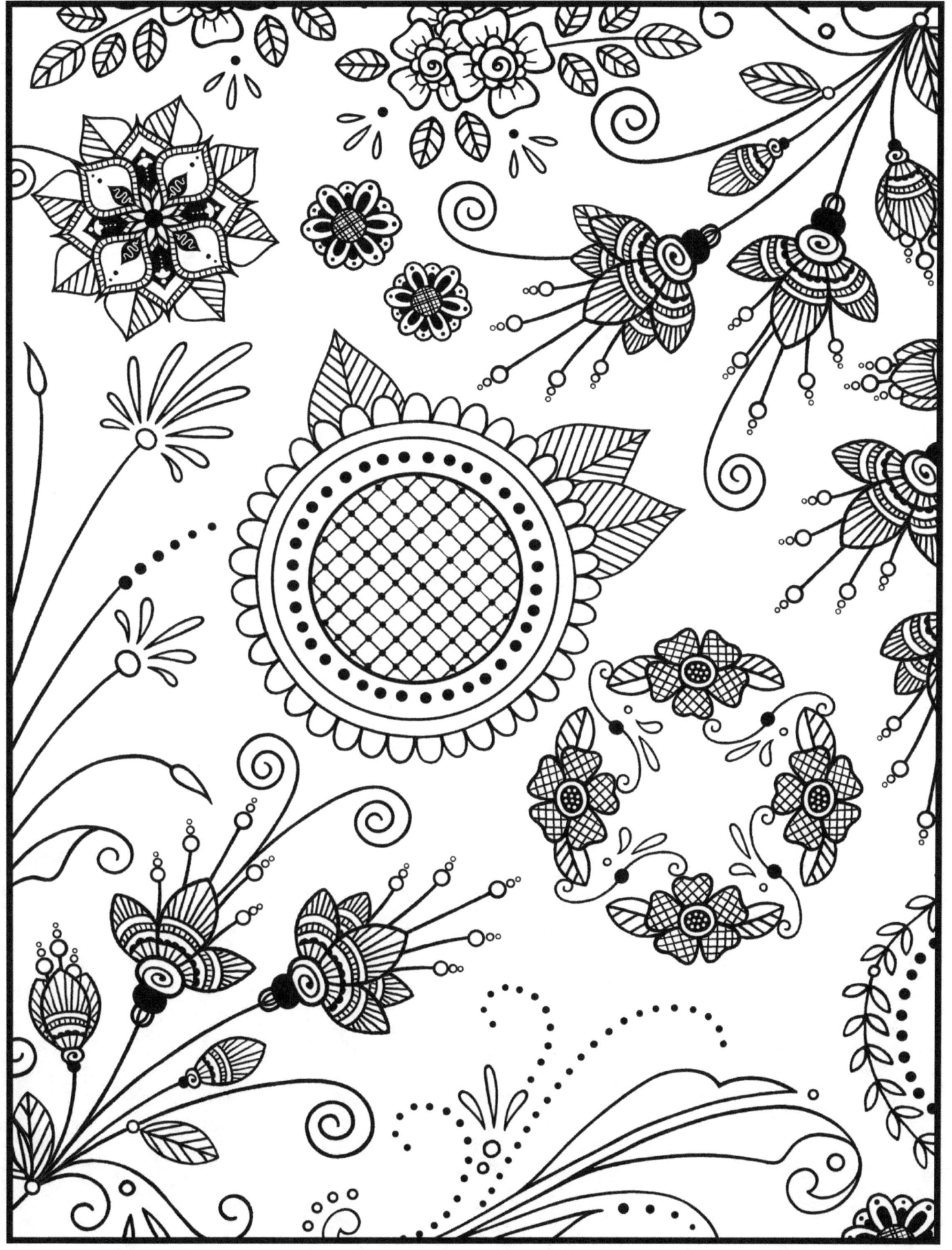

About the Author

Olivia A Kneibler is an internationally known artist who has been creating her whimsical illustrations for years. She has worked with companies such as DecoArt, pcCrafter, Bradford Exchange, Gibson Greetings, Paper Magic Group, Annette Funicello Collectible Bear Company, Leisure Arts, and Race Point Publishing. With the experience gathered over her career she founded Olivia and Co., an online shop. Now, Olivia is including books to her creative endeavors and is busy creating her new website Alexandrienne, which will offer coloring pages, coloring books, craft books, journals, and more.

Art has been her passion since she was a very young girl. She majored in fine art and psychology in college and is a veteran of the United States Air Force. She has four wonderful sons and grandchildren who have encouraged her to pursue her passion.

Acknowledgements

I would like to extend my sincerest gratitude to everyone who helped to make this book not just a possibility but a reality; to everyone who provided support, from proofreading to funding.

I would like to thank my entire family for the many helpful conversations about the book, proofreading, design input, having patience with the late nights, and so much more. A special thanks to my youngest son, Chase, who believed in me and helped me throughout this entire process.

To all of my friends, thank you. Your emails of encouragement, support, ideas, and recognition have kept me positive throughout these months which helped to give me the belief that I could accomplish this goal.

A special thank you to Johanne, Kara, Karen, Thena, and the rest of my contributors, your financial support has enabled me to go forward with the publishing of this book. It would have been impossible without you and for this I am deeply grateful.

A Note From the Author

There are a lot of coloring books on the market so when I decided to do another book after, The Art of Drawing Dangles, I wanted it to be special. Being an adult is stressful; coloring has been shown to have calming effects on children and adults. One of my goals was for this book to be fun, but also to provide needed stress relief. I wanted artwork that challenged those that love intricate designs, but was light hearted and whimsical for those that just wanted to relax. I also wanted pages that could be removed from the book and framed, or given as gifts when they were finished. I hope, in this book, that I have found that balance. I loved creating this book, the thought of who would have this book in their home, and what they would create with it. That is the motivation behind my art, and it has been for a very long time. Nothing gives me more pleasure than seeing what people have done with my art or hearing that it brought them joy. Together, we can make this world a more cohesive and loving place one color at a time.

This is my personal invitation to share your experiences with me and other coloring enthusiasts. You can join us at Art with Olivia A Kneibler Facebook Group and www.instagram.com/oliviaakneibler.

If you have any questions, comments, and/or suggestions please don't hesitate to contact me at olivia@oliviaandco.com, I would love to hear from you.

Other Books and Products by Olivia

The Art of Drawing Dangles: Creating Decorative Letters and Art with Charms

Published by: Race Point Publishing

Dangles is a whimsical art form that lends itself wonderfully to lettering, tangling, and many other types of art. Let your imagination guide you while you explore the possibilities. This book has 50 projects including the upper and lower case alphabet as well as many other creative images to help you learn how to dangle. Before long you will be able to create your own charming dangled cards, coloring pages, images to frame, stationery, journal pages and so much more. Available wherever books are sold.

www.oliviaandco.com - Downloadable artwork created by Olivia

www.alexandrienne.com - Is coming soon and will contain coloring pages, coloring books, instructions books, and more created by Olivia.

www.ingramcontent.com/pod-product-compliance
Lightning Source LLC
Chambersburg PA
CBHW080818170526
45158CB00009B/2463

* 9 7 8 0 9 9 9 5 6 8 6 0 6 *